STOP-PRAY -

With careful research and keen insig. ... ...que perspective as a woman writing for women about a most extraordinary woman— one whom God used in a most special way in His plan of salvation for all nations, even when God may have seemed far away.

Andrew H. Bartelt, professor emeritus of exegetical theology, Concordia Seminary

Author Donna Snow brings her engaging trademark charm, humor, and insights to this study on the Book of Esther. Grab your Bible and be ready to search as Donna takes us all through the Scriptures with personal, practical applications for our daily walk with Jesus. I was richly blessed by doing this study, and I am honored to be asked to endorse it. Readers will not be disappointed.

Janice Wendorf, 16th president, Lutheran Women's Missionary League

Donna Snow's latest Bible study on the Book of Esther is deep, thought-provoking, and spiritually challenging. Though the culture of Esther is vastly different from our times today, there is much relevance in the pressures that modern women face and the same sovereign hope that gives us identical courage to face our greatest fears and wildest destinies!

Jessica R. Patch, best-selling author of the Seasons of Hope series

Chosen: A Study of Esther reaches hearts that ache for God's help. Donna Snow leads us on a poignant, edifying, scholarly, insightful, and fun journey through one of the most fascinating accounts in Scripture. This Christ-centered study reveals the true God who doesn't seek the limelight but who walks with the least of these to accomplish His miraculous rescue and dole out His lavish grace.

Rev. Michael Newman, president of the Texas District, LCMS,
and author of *Hope When Your Heart Breaks: Navigating Grief and Loss*

Donna Snow has been our guest on the Family Shield radio program many times. It is always a joy and a privilege for me to interview her. She is an exceptional Bible study teacher and a wonderful author who shares God's Word, the Gospel of Christ, and who encourages Christians to grow in faith. Her well-researched Bible studies make the people of God's Word come alive. We learn how they dealt with many challenges and served the Lord. I highly recommend her new Bible study, *Chosen: A Study of Esther.*

Kay L. Meyer, president and host, Family Shield Ministries

Who doesn't love the fairy-tale-like story of Esther—an orphan turned queen? This Old Testament book has long been a favorite of mine, and I have studied it in-depth several times, yet Donna Snow's study, *Chosen*, gave me new perspectives. The book delves into the history of Esther yet offers applications for our modern-day lives. It tells the seemingly hopeless story of Jews facing destruction yet points out how God used a young Jewish girl to reverse that destruction. Most important, *Chosen* reminds us that when our situation appears desperate and God seems hidden, the Lord continues to work for our good behind the scenes.

Sharla Fritz, author of *God's Relentless Love*

Get ready for a great Bible study on the Book of Esther. Frankly, it will be hard to put it down before you finish it! Donna Snow brings this compelling story of God's love for His chosen people, the Jews, to life as it plays out as if being performed on a Broadway stage. Intrigue, love, hate, forgiveness, stepping out of one's comfort zone, and much more will draw you into this study of God's Word. You will come away with a much better understanding of how God is always involved in the lives of those He loves, both Jews and Gentiles!

Rev. Dr. Robert M. Roegner, liaison to Israel, Apple of His Eye Mission Society

In her latest study, *Chosen*, Donna Snow leads with one foot firmly planted in biblical history and investigation and one in the core message of God's grace for us in Jesus Christ. Donna's friendly tone invites the reader into the palace of the kings of Persia and into the life of a young woman named Esther to work through questions relevant to our lives today, including leadership and authority, God's timing, and the value of human life. Rather than sequestering Esther to simply a woman before a king, as Ahasuerus's beauty pageant did so long ago, Donna expands our vantage point to see the powerful role Esther, Mordecai, and others like them played in the narrative of

Christ's salvation for His people throughout time.

Heidi Goehmann, mental health advocate and author, LCSW, deaconess

In this fantastic new study, Donna shows how God has great purpose for each of us. He isn't as interested in our ability as our availability, and Esther, through her obedient sacrifice, was available to God at a critical time, saving many lives. With incredible research and impressive detail, Donna shows us the fingerprints of God's redemptive plan, pointing us to Jesus. It is a challenging and convicting study as it draws on God's Word, promising an exciting and transformational plunge into the Book of Esther and beyond, reminding us that God calls us for such a time as this!

Rev. Dr. Gregory S. Walton, president, Florida-Georgia District, LCMS

In her new Bible study, *Chosen*, Donna Snow provides a carefully researched and insightful study of the Book of Esther. Rich with historical context and Snow's hard-earned wisdom, *Chosen* reminds us that the beautiful Jewish Esther was forced into a beauty contest. Snow uses a movie metaphor to help readers understand the king's values, how he ran his opulent court, and the dangerous times. She uses other Scripture passages to deepen the reader's understanding and reminds us that without even mentioning God's name, the Book of Esther shows us God's hand was apparent in its monumental events.

Michelle Ule, women's Bible study leader, St. Mark Lutheran Church, Santa Rosa, CA

Donna Snow skillfully leads readers into a thoughtful, in-depth study of this timeless drama. The true tale of a Jewish-girl-turned-Persian-queen, the Book of Esther reveals the unlikely influence of one faith-filled, courageous woman. The Lord works mightily backstage as the drama of His displaced people unfolds, builds, then comes to a climax when He delivers them from certain death, thereby preserving the promised remnant from which Christ would come. Through this powerful study, you'll be inspired to rise up and recognize God's work in and through you, as He emboldens you to live out His plan and purpose "for such a time as this" (Esther 4:14). Like Esther, you have been chosen in your time for faith-filled, influential witness to a watching world. You, too, can reveal the Lord's glory through courageous, God-honoring decisions. Today, as then, He moves through

His people, often in unlikely situations, to bring about deliverance—from death to life—in Christ.

Donna Snow's *Chosen* will rock your world in the best way. With sound theology and a warm conversational tone, this study is easy to dig into and will bring you a wealth of information and insight into the character of God and why He has chosen you. Highly recommend!

In this study of Esther, Donna not only gives us the historical context and the play-by-play of the dramatic story, but she always points us back to Jesus, the real hero in all of our lives. This book will keep you on the edge of your seat as Donna points out historical details and helps us dig deep into God's precious Word. Grab your study Bible, your highlighters, and a pen, and get ready to take lots of notes because this study was made for such a time as this.

CHOSEN
A STUDY OF ESTHER

DONNA SNOW

CONCORDIA PUBLISHING HOUSE • SAINT LOUIS

Published by Concordia Publishing House
3558 S. Jefferson Ave., St. Louis, MO 63118–3968
1-800-325-3040 • cph.org

Manufactured in the United States of America

3 4 5 6 7 8 9 10 11 12   30 29 28 27 26 25 24 23 22 21

DEDICATION

To Luanne Walling, Belinda Burmeister, and Linda Gage:
Thank you for being vibrant examples of Esther's strength, courage,
and bravery in my life. I love you.

CONTENTS

Introduction to Our Study of Esther

Welcome to an epic cinematic drama as the curtain rises over a Jewish girl caught in circumstances beyond her control. Time after time, the invisible hand of God intervenes in her life and in the life of her people to save them from certain annihilation.

The story opens amid the lavish setting of a royal pagan feast in the capital of the opulent Persian Empire. After dismissing his queen for disobedience, King Ahasuerus demands that all of the beautiful young virgins be paraded before him as new-wife material.

Esther is swept into the king's palace, and we get a front-row seat. Over time, Esther finds favor with the king and is eventually crowned queen. Throughout Esther's time in the palace, Mordecai, her cousin and guardian, provides wise counsel, which she carefully follows.

When the evil court official Haman sets his mind to eradicate the Jewish people from Persia, it becomes clear that God has positioned Esther center stage to wield her influence with the king in order to rescue God's children from genocide. As the story dramatically unfolds, the Book of Esther paints a masterpiece portrait of the providence of God.

In a book about God, it should be a prerequisite that the text makes some mention of Him. However, the Book of Esther never mentions God, but He is everywhere—swaying a kingdom for the sake of His kingdom. And the way God turns the tables is spectacular.

Esther's story easily compares to an invisible chess game between God and Satan, where God inevitably declares, "Checkmate!" Esther is part of an oppressed people living in a foreign land. She was an orphan with a lot of character but not a lot of opportunities.

As we study her journey, you and I will see how the character of Esther imitates the character of Christ. Esther lost her parents and came from a foster home to a place of royalty. Jesus appeared to be conceived out of wedlock (of course, we know better) and came from a town in obscurity to a place of royalty.

At God's appointed time, Esther revealed her true identity and leveraged her position to save Israel. At God's appointed time, Jesus revealed His true identity and leveraged His life to save mankind.

This comprehensive study provides clear biblical direction on how we have been chosen, equipped, and given God's perfect counsel from Scripture to step out as culture-changers. However, fear often inhibits our forward momentum. Esther struggles with fear as well.

Esther inspires us to determine where we put our focus. We can choose to look back on childhood shortcomings as an excuse not to act, or we can look to future opportunities that God has already prepared for us.

The Book of Esther was written to the Jewish exiles to encourage their faith with reminders of God's faithfulness as their holy Promise Keeper. God uses Esther's story to open our eyes to a much bigger view of Himself and helps us understand that every decision He leads us to make sets the stage for His glory to shine bright.

Through the inspiration of the Holy Spirit, the author of Esther reveals God's movements and His covenant relationship with His people. The text reveals how the hiddenness of God does not mean the absence of God.

In God's flawless timing, He guides Esther's path to preserve the Jews and eventually brings forth a Savior in the land of His choosing "when the fullness of time had come" (Galatians 4:4).

I applaud you for embarking on this Bible study adventure! As you open your Bible to Esther's story, my fervent prayer is that God engages all five senses to the vivid colors and dramatic sounds of courage, faith, and grace. In this complex, elaborate drama, I pray that God ultimately reveals His unwavering, dramatic love for you, dear sister in Christ.

Timeline and the Achaemenid Dynasty's Line of Kings

Date	Event(s)
538 BC	Cyrenian Decree: Cyrus, king of Persia, signs a decree allowing Jews to return to their homeland
485	Ahasuerus (Ahasuerus I) becomes Persia's king
483	Ahasuerus throws a lavish 180-day feast in Susa, followed by 7-day feast for all
482–479	Ahasuerus led the Persians in several failed attempts to invade Greece
479	Ahasuerus' officials hold nationwide search for new queen
479–478	Esther crowned as Persia's new queen
April 474	Haman despises Mordecai for not bowing; determines to destroy all Persian Jews
April 17, 474	Haman casts lots (pur) and sets date for the Jewish genocide to occur on March 7, 473 (eleven months in the future)
June 474	Esther foils Haman's plot; Ahasuerus orders Haman's execution
June 25, 474	Ahasuerus allows Esther and Mordecai to issue royal decree enabling Jews to defend themselves against genocide
March 7, 474	Jews successfully defend themselves against Persian forces
March 8, 474	Haman's ten sons are hanged; Jews celebrate battle victories; 500 Persians killed in Susa
March 9, 474	Jews celebrate victory in Susa Achaemenid Dynasty
550–529 BC	Cyrus the Great
529–522 BC	Cambyses I
522–486 BC	Darius I (the Great)
486–465 BC	Ahasuerus I (Ahasuerus)
465–425 BC	Artaxerxes I (Nehemiah served as cupbearer)
425–424 BC	Ahasuerus II
424–405 BC	Darius II
405–359 BC	Artaxerxes II
359–338 BC	Artaxerxes III
338–336 BC	Arses (also known as Artaxerxes IV)
336–300 BC	Darius III

Challenges in Studying the Book of Esther

The word *king* appears more than one hundred times, and the proper name of the king (whether Ahasuerus or Xerxes) appears nearly three dozen times, yet God is not mentioned even once. This practice followed a trend among the exiles and the generations that followed never to speak God's name, which meant they could never misuse it (violating the Second Commandment) and be punished again by exile. To this day, when Jews come across "YHWH," they speak the name "Lord" or "Adonai." You can see hints of this in the Gospels when the Jews speak of "the Highest" or "the Blessed One" because they are going out of their way not to say God's name. Regardless of the absence of His name, God is this drama's unmistakable leading Man.

God works behind the scenes to faithfully preserve Israel's remnant. If God wanted the author to reveal Him by name, He certainly could have brought it about. God was not hiding; His name was merely hidden.

Scholar A. H. Sayce wrote:

> In the Book of Esther the Divine name does not occur even once; and we look in vain for references to religious observants—fasting perhaps excepted—and even to the peculiar institutions of the Jews. Nevertheless, secular as it seems to be in tone, it has been made an instrument through which God has revealed His will to us, and prepared the way for the work of Christ.[1]

A number of Protestant reformers, including Martin Luther, disliked the Book of Esther. Specifically, one comment attributed to Luther: "I am so hostile to the book [2 Maccabees] and to Esther that I wish they did not exist at all; for they judaize too much, and have much heathen perverseness."[2] Other scholars point to the lack of references to God, Jerusalem or its temple, and traditional religious Israelite practices.

Other scholars question its inclusion in the canon since Esther was the only Old Testament book not found among the Dead Sea Scrolls. The Dead Sea Scrolls (written between 250 BC and AD 50) discovered at Qumran from 1946 to 1956 have authenticated the vast majority of the Hebrew Bible. Recent advances in technology have now revealed that unidentified scroll fragments originally uncovered at Qumran contain the Book of Esther. Several unidentified fragments were wine-soaked and stuck together, previously making them impossible to read. New technology now offers scientists the ability to look through the stains to determine a fragment's contents.[3] Because of this modern technology, parts from *all* books in the Hebrew Bible—including Esther—have been positively identified. Praise the Lord!

Why is such a discovery important? The Dead Sea Scrolls at Qumran confirm that God's Word is true and unchanging—as applicable thousands of years ago as it is today.

Even though scholars questioned Esther's inclusion in the biblical canon, diligent disciples apply ourselves to learn what God teaches in *all* of the Bible's pages. Why? "All Scripture is breathed out by God and profitable for teaching, for reproof, for correction, and for training in righteousness, that the man of God may be complete, equipped for every good work" (2 Timothy 3:16–17).

The Bible is our ultimate authority over all matters (Matthew 5:18; John 10:35). Scripture is the incomparable source of our knowledge of God and assurance of the hope of salvation provided through Jesus Christ (John 5:39–47). It is a believer's essential resource for navigating everyday life (1 Peter 2:2).

Esther was included in the canon because of its acceptance in both Judaism and the Christian Church, as well as its illuminating worth of showing God's providential care of His chosen people (Romans 9–11; Revelation 7; 14).

The *Lutheran Bible Companion* sums it up nicely:

> In both Genesis and Esther, it was not a blind, capricious force but
> a force that "in all things" deliberately let God "work together for
> good, for those" for whom it shaped events (Romans 8:28). This
> force could not be stymied by forces of evil, even if they repre-

sented the resources of a world empire. It established a universal tribunal of justice where right and wrong have their day in court. This often unnamed power is "the finger of God"

(Exodus 8:19; Luke 11:20).[4]

So where do we find the Gospel in the Book of Esther? In God's divine providence. He uses Esther to deliver His people, thereby preserving the line through which our Savior Jesus Christ would come forth.

Helpful Insights for Our Study

REVERSALS OF FORTUNE: CHIASTIC STRUCTURE

One of the most well-known themes throughout the Book of Esther is a chiastic structure reflecting reversals of fortune. The word *chiasm* is derived from the Greek letter *chi*, which looks like our letter X. Chiasms provide a mirror effect as ideas are reflected in reverse order. A common chiasm is "When the going gets tough, the tough get going."

The Book of Esther contains many chiasms, such as when Haman erects gallows on which to hang Mordecai, only to be hung on them himself. And, of course, an important chiasm is when Esther risks her own life to save the lives of all Persian Jews.

BANQUETS AND FEASTS

Feasting, celebrating, and drinking comprise a prominent feature in the Book of Esther. Each feast cues a significant reversal of fortune in the storyline. In fact, due to the sheer number of feasts, some scholars structure their entire biblical study of the book around the feasting timeline. Almost half of the appearances of the Hebrew word for *banquet* (מִשְׁתֶּה, *mishteh*) in the Bible are found in the Book of Esther. As each feast appears throughout this study, we will savor its importance.

Here's a quick reference list:

Scripture Location	Feast Event
Esther 1:1–4	Ahasuerus's 180-day banquet to display wealth and power
Esther 1:5	Ahasuerus's 7-day banquet for all of Susa
Esther 1:9	Queen Vashti holds feast for women
Esther 2:18	Banquet given for Esther as Persia's new queen
Esther 3:15	Ahasuerus and Haman celebrate signing decree to annihilate the Jews
Esther 5:5–8	Esther's first banquet for Ahasuerus and Haman
Esther 7:1–3	Esther's second banquet for Ahasuerus and Haman, where she exposes Haman as architect of genocide
Esther 8:15–16	Mordecai honored for appointment as prime minister
Esther 9:17	First Jewish banquet of Purim
Esther 9:18	Second Jewish banquet of Purim

GOD'S SOVEREIGNTY AND OVERARCHING MESSAGE

The Book of Esther demonstrates that God is sovereign over all things, even seemingly insignificant events. We read the Book of Esther hearing Romans 8:28 ring loud: "And we know that for those who love God all things work together for good, for those who are called according to His purpose."

In his famous poem "The Present Crisis," James Russell Lowell penned these words:

Careless seems the great Avenger; history's pages but record

One death-grapple in the darkness 'twixt old systems and the Word;

Truth forever on the scaffold, Wrong forever on the throne.

Yet that scaffold sways the future, and, behind the dim unknown,

Standeth God within the shadow, keeping watch above his own.[5]

HISTORY

Two Old Testament books, Esther and Exodus, recount how God faithfully preserved His chosen people against all foreign powers that attempted to savagely annihilate the Jews (according to His covenant promise to Abraham). The events recorded in Esther fall between chapters 6 and 7 of the Book of Ezra and close out the Old Testament's historical section. Only Ezra 7–10, Nehemiah, and Malachi report Old Testament history later than Esther.

Across the board, scholars agree that Esther's author possessed intimate knowledge of Persian etiquette, customs, and history, as well as familiarity with Susa's winter palace (1:5–7). Interestingly, the author also possessed detailed knowledge of the Hebrew calendar and customs and a deep-seated view of Jewish nationalism.

After Cyrus the Great's decree released the Israelites from exile (this time is referred to as the postexilic period, from 539 to about 332 BC), many Jews chose to stay where they were. This brings up an important question: By remaining in a pagan land, did they forfeit their inheritance as God's covenant people?

The Book of Esther answers that question beautifully as we see God positioning people and coordinating circumstances to again protect and rescue His chosen people. Through them, God remains faithful to His covenant to accomplish His perfect plan of redemption for all who believe by faith.

ESTHER'S GLOBAL MESSAGE FOR OUR PRESENT DAY

There is much to glean from the Book of Esther about living in exile, specifically in countries where believers and the Church are relentlessly persecuted. God's Church now covers the globe and exists in many places that are hostile to it. Even in the United States, we operate under leaders who may or may not follow scriptural authority on many important issues.

A quick read through the Book of Acts reveals how often believers and the Church navigated life under pagan rule. One only need to look to Nero and other leaders who regularly sought to destroy the "Jesus" movement.

The apostle Peter, who understood persecution firsthand, writes how those in the global Church are "elect exiles of the Dispersion" (1 Peter 1:1) and "sojourners and exiles" (1 Peter 2:11). We are exiles in the very land that we will inherit, though now it lies broken and fallen. All believers will celebrate liberation and renewal when all things that God promised through Christ come to pass (Romans 8:18–25; Philippians 3:20–21).

God faithfully protects and preserves His covenant people. The Book of Esther is a favorite among today's Jewish community because it reminds them of God's promises and Abraham's faith.

THE APOCRYPHA

In the late second or early first century BC, the Septuagint (Greek translation of the Old Testament Hebrew Bible) produced six additional passages in the Book of Esther that were not adopted as part of our biblical canon. Jerome, a Christian scholar, revised the Old Latin translation of the Bible and collected these additional passages and added them to the end of the canonical book.

Protestants (following Martin Luther's lead) traditionally label these additions apocryphal. In Protestant Bibles, they are usually printed in a separate section apart from the canon. Their purpose was to add specific religious elements (such as prayer), intensify dramatic interest, and authenticate the books' events. Within the Apocrypha's pages for the Book of Esther, God is mentioned more than fifty times, Jewish customs and traditions are included, and so is Esther's loathing of her pagan surroundings. We will look at these additions as they occur in the timeline of our study.

THE THREE TEXTS OF THE BOOK OF ESTHER

Among the distinguished women in Scripture, only Esther and Ruth appear as books in the Bible. The story of Esther is told in three different ancient texts:

1. Masoretic Text = original Hebrew text
2. Septuagint = Greek translation of original Hebrew that also includes the Apocrypha (or six additions), preserved in four medieval manuscripts
3. Alpha Text = a second Greek translation

One of the most glaring contrasts is that the Apocrypha portrays Esther as a meek, prayerful woman who even faints when she stands uninvited before Ahasuerus. However, the Masoretic text displays Esther as bold and fearless, courageously facing every challenge.

The Jewish Bible, the *Tanakh,* is divided into three sections: (1) Torah, the Books of Moses (or the Law); (2) the Nevi'im, the Book of the Prophets; and (3) Ketuvim, the Writings. Esther falls in the Ketuvim, which is comprised of eleven books. One subset of these includes Song of Songs, Ruth, Lamentations, Ecclesiastes, and Esther. Collectively, these are known as the *Megillot* or *Five Scrolls.*

Jesus refers to this division in Luke 24:44 on the evening of Easter: "everything written about Me in the Law of Moses and the Prophets and the Psalms must be fulfilled."

As you open God's incredible Word, I believe that He has led you to this study for such a time as this. Will you take a moment in prayer as you approach Scripture with this study? Ask God to give you an open, receptive heart. He plants rich seeds of faith in such fertile soil.

On a personal note, for more than two years, God has been stirring and preparing me to write this in-depth study on the Book of Esther. He turns my soul upside down each time He inspires me to open His Word. I fervently pray that He will do the same for you. Such a stirring means that He is working on us from the inside out to make us more like Jesus.

The Book of Esther has profoundly impacted my spiritual journey. It taught me invaluable lessons about being a secure woman of God in a world that judges a women's exterior as the sum total and moves on. Esther was beautiful, but that beauty penetrated to her very soul as she risked her life to save an entire race.

I pray that God ignites a fire in your soul to be a continuous student of the Word. There is nothing else that has transformed my heart so completely as getting lost in Bible study for hours at a time. I wish I could sit by you and study this together. I pray that you gather a group of women to join you on this adventure. To talk about what God is revealing. To be shocked at the evil that can exist in the human heart. To shed tears as God reveals the sacrificial love of Jesus.

Finally, I invite you to turn your mind and heart to the epic, historical story called the Book of Esther.

An Opulent Stage

ESTHER 1

The curtain opens to reveal the colorful, flamboyant setting of the Persian capital of Susa. As King Ahasuerus throws lavish banquets to gain support for his military campaigns against Greece, Queen Vashti occupies her time throwing her own banquet. Their respective parties are going well—until the king invites the queen to join him.

- **DAY 1**   In the Days of Ahasuerus *(Esther 1:1–2)*
- **DAY 2**   Ahasuerus Throws a Party *(Esther 1:3–4)*
- **DAY 3**   Banquets and Persian Opulence *(Esther 1:5–8)*
- **DAY 4**   Queen Vashti: The Choice Women Face *(Esther 1:9–12)*
- **DAY 5**   Manipulating Weak Leaders *(Esther 1:13–22)*

KEY QUESTIONS

- Are you easily swayed by opulence?
- What reversal of fortunes have you experienced in your life? How have you handled them?
- Empire-building took center stage in the king of Persia's life. What sits in the center of yours?

DAY 1
In the Days of Ahasuerus

Now in the days of Ahasuerus, the Ahasuerus who reigned from India to Ethiopia over 127 provinces, in those days when King Ahasuerus sat on his royal throne in Susa, the citadel.

(Esther 1:1–2)

Like any cinematic-worthy drama, the Book of Esther weaves an epic tale of good versus evil, heroine versus villain, and sacrifice versus avarice. The author begins with a wide-angle lens and slowly closes in as Esther's plot thickens. Several years span the first two chapters alone. Yet for the rest of the book, the camera lens narrows to only one year. In some places, the lens captures only a few days.

KING AHASUERUS

Ahasuerus was the son of Darius I (Darius the Great, 522–486 BC) and Queen Atossa, daughter of Cyrus the Great. He was the fourth legitimate monarch in the Achaemenid Empire, which ruled over Persia for more than 175 years, beginning with Cyrus the Great until Persia was conquered by Alexander the Great. Following the death of his father, Darius the Great, in November 486, Ahasuerus reigned over the Persian Empire until 465 BC.

Due to his illustrious lineage, the king is most widely recognized by his Greek name, Xerxes. His Persian name was Khshayarsha, from which was derived the Hebrew translation of Ahasuerus, which we use throughout this study.

Archaeological records have portrayed Ahasuerus as weak-willed and self-centered in domestic affairs and easily swayed by manipulative, sycophant courtiers. As we will discover in Esther, Haman fit this description perfectly as he manipulated Ahasuerus to order the annihilation of the Jewish population. However, on the battlefield, Ahasuerus was a forceful leader who fiercely chased his goals.

Read Esther 1:1–2.

What does Esther 1:1 reveal about Ahasuerus?

Ahasuerus ruled over the vast Persian Empire, which was the dominant world power in Esther's day. It spanned 127 provinces and thousands of square miles from northwest India, across the ancient Near East (including all of Asia Minor), and into northern Africa. This far-reaching land was divided into numerous provinces governed by satraps.

After the Babylonians destroyed Jerusalem's temple and laid waste to the Kingdom of Judah around 587–586 BC, a substantial number of remaining Jews, including Esther's Israelite ancestors, were taken into Babylonian exile. Then, after conquering the Babylonians, around 539 BC, the Persian Empire came into power under the rule of Cyrus the Great. This period is referred to as the Achaemenid Persian Empire (to avoid confusing it with later, smaller empires in Persia). The Achaemenid Persian Empire eventually became one of the largest empires in the ancient world—surpassing Alexander's Empire and even the mighty Roman Empire afterward.

The Greek researcher and historian Herodotus of Halicarnassus (480–429 BC) is a valuable resource that provides first-person insight into the Persian Empire during the reign of Ahasuerus and the events of the Book of Esther. He wrote *The Histories,* which chronicle the Persian Wars around 445 BC, including King Ahasuerus's reign.

Herodotus details the expansion of the Achaemenid Empire under its various rulers, which culminated in Ahasuerus's disastrous naval battle against Greece in 480 BC, along with the engagements at Plataea and Mycale.

Fifty years before the events of the Book of Esther, Cyrus ruled over Persia and passed a life-changing decree concerning the Israelites.

According to Ezra 1:1–4, what did Cyrus decree?

Despite Cyrus's decree, many Jews chose to remain in Babylon, where they had prospered, rather than face unknown prospects in a war-ravaged Judean land. The first six chapters of the Book of Ezra tell the story of the first returned exiles. The building of the second temple occurred during this time. The Jews who chose to remain in the land of their captivity following their freedom are known as Diaspora Jews. The second half of the Book of Daniel is also a Diaspora story.

Some freed Judeans traveled even farther west and settled in Susa, where they discovered opportunities to prosper and attain influential positions. Nehemiah, a former exiled Jew, is a perfect example of success because he became cupbearer for Ahasuerus's son, King Artaxerxes I.

For reasons not specifically revealed in the biblical authority, the ancestors of Esther and Mordecai (Esther's older cousin) chose to remain in Persia and settle in Susa, where we witness the lion's share of Esther's story.

SUSA, THE CITADEL

One of four royal cities, Susa was located approximately two hundred miles east of Babylon in what is now southern Iraq. It sprawled over two miles on three hills overlooking the Shaur River. On an elevated area on the northern point of Susa, Darius built a ten-acre citadel (or castle) to accommodate the royal court during Persia's winter months. The citadel subsequently housed many of his successors, including Ahasuerus.

Excavations of Susa's citadel have uncovered features that reveal much about court life. Archaeologists have uncovered an audience hall, which was a square building that stretched more than 350 feet on every side and boasted dozens of stone columns ranging from 65 to 80 feet tall.

As we read through Esther, it is easy to imagine the opulence surrounding King Ahasuerus, who had the world at his feet. At his winter palace in Susa, sumptuous feasts and glittering wealth served as the lavish backdrop of Ahasuerus and his extensive court.

Yet all of Susa's magnificence and luxury cannot hide the ugly heart of Esther's story: the very real threat of the unmitigated slaughter of God's chosen people.

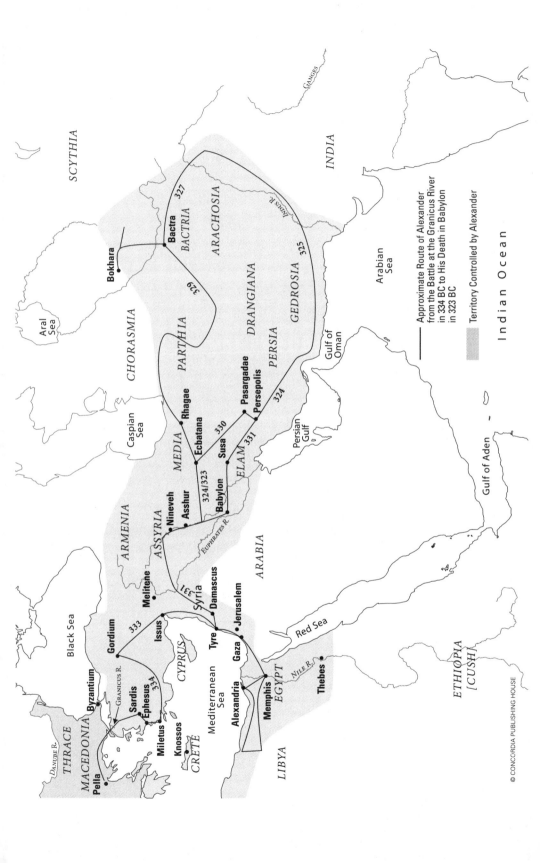

SCYTHIA

GANGES

INDIA

327

BACTRA

Bokhara

BACTRIA

ARACHOSIA

INDUS R.

325

Arabian
Sea

Approximate Route of Alexander
from the Battle at the Granicus River
in 334 BC to His Death in Babylon
in 323 BC

Territory Controlled by Alexander

I n d i a n   O c e a n

Aral
Sea

CHORASMIA

329

PARTHIA

DRANGIANA

PERSIA

GEDROSIA

Gulf of
Oman

Caspian
Sea

Rhagae

Pasargadae

Persepolis

324

Ecbatana

330

MEDIA

Susa

ELAM 331

Persian
Gulf

324/323

Nineveh

Asshur

Babylon

ARMENIA

ASSYRIA

EUPHRATES R.

ARABIA

Gulf of Aden

Melitene

331

Damascus

Jerusalem

Syria

333

Gordium

Issus

Tyre

Red Sea

Black Sea

GRANICUS R.

Sardis

Ephesus

334

CYPRUS

Gaza

Jerusalem

NILE R.

ETHIOPIA
[CUSH]

THRACE

Byzantium

MACEDONIA

Pella

DANUBE R.

Miletus

Knossos

CRETE

Mediterranean
Sea

Alexandria

Memphis

EGYPT

Thebes

LIBYA

© CONCORDIA PUBLISHING HOUSE

God performed numerous miracles on behalf of the Israelites to free them from slavery in Egypt and captivity in Babylon. Sometimes, God works through miracles; other times, He works miracles through ordinary people. That *is* the miracle. Esther's meager beginnings could never have foreshadowed how her life of royalty would unfold. Yet God knew.

What does Ephesians 1:11 tell us?

If you are in Christ, you are an heir to a matchless inheritance! What is that inheritance? Eternal life as His heirs, saved through faith in Jesus Christ. In a word, heaven.

Ahasuerus inherited a mighty kingdom because his father was Persia's king. Believers in Jesus Christ inherit a kingdom that cannot be shaken because our heavenly Father is the King of kings.

How does knowing what you will inherit by faith change how you live today?

If your earthly father was a billionaire and you knew that one day you would inherit all of that wealth, how would it change the way you live today?

LITERARY GENRE

While some scholars classify Esther in the historical literary genre, it has also been classified as Diaspora literature, a court tale, a Jewish novella, wisdom court legend, and an exaggerated tale. Interestingly, the absence of any mention of God is a powerful literary device that causes readers to recognize God on each page.

Along with chiasms, the literary tool of doubling also occurs in the Book of Esther. For instance, Queen Vashti resisted a royal command that provoked action against all women, and Mordecai resisted a royal command that provoked action against all Jews.

I found this quote particularly helpful:

> Given all the literary features of the Book of Esther, the Christian must decide how to approach this book of the Bible. Is it just a story? Is it history? Just what is it? What we think about the book will determine how we read it, and how we read it will determine what we can learn from it. Our presuppositions—that is, what we bring to the reading of this book—are extremely important.[6]

BACK TO THE STORY

The Book of Esther starts with which five words?

"Now in the days of" almost sounds like the start of a fairy tale: *"Once upon a time."* Other historical books such as Joshua, Judges, and 1 and 2 Samuel contain similar openings. This was simply a literary tool used by the author to announce that the following story is based on actual events.

For instance, compare Star Wars, "A long time ago in a galaxy far, far away" with the opening words of Luke 2: "In those days a decree went out from Caesar Augustus that all the world should be registered." Luke went on to specify which of Augustus's three census decrees this was: "This was the first [of two] registration when Quirinius was governor of Syria" (2:2). This sets the events as historical reality in a definite period of history.

So as we begin our journey through the palace hallways in Esther, I pray that God grants you the ears to hear and eyes to see His providential grace throughout.

DAY 2
Ahasuerus Throws a Party

> In the third year of his reign he gave a feast for all his officials and servants. The army of Persia and Media and the nobles and governors of the provinces were before him, while he showed the riches of his royal glory and the splendor and pomp of his greatness for many days, 180 days.
>
> (Esther 1:3–4)

The director's camera now widens to reveal the extraordinary palace of King Ahasuerus in Susa. The multisensory glitz, splendor, and pomp of his court must have rivaled Hollywood on steroids. It was champagne wishes and caviar dreams at every glance.

Read Esther 1:3–4.

How many days was the king's lavish party?

Can you imagine a six-month-long party? What level of planning would that require?

I love welcoming family and friends to my home to share life over shared meals, but it would last more like six hours, not months. Women tend to be the party organizers for family functions. Just think about the expense, the preparation, and *the cleanup!* I don't know about you, but my eyes just glazed over at the sheer planning aspect. There really can be too much of a good thing.

According to Esther 1:3, who attended the banquet?

Historians estimate that thousands took turns dining with Ahasuerus during those 180 days. Ahasuerus's empire was as diverse as it was vast. Many ethnicities, languages, and religions called Persia home because Persia had conquered many nations, including Babylon and the nations it had conquered, which included Assyria and the many nations it had conquered. Competing in the shadow of his father, Ahasuerus desired to expand Persia even more.

The king needed to demonstrate to his financial and political backers that he possessed the resources to wage a successful war. He had his sights set on conquering Greece (instead of making it a trade partner) in order to boost the royal treasuries and expand trade prospects.

With such a diverse population, Ahasuerus needed to spread out the banquet to allow time for each guest from each people group to attend.

King Ahasuerus liked to flaunt his wealth to make a case for war. What does the Bible say in the following verses about properly understanding and handling wealth?

Proverbs 30:7–9

- give me poverty nor riches

Proverbs 31:20

Whether in plenty or poverty, what encouragement or challenge does God provide in these verses for you today?

God provides for our every need. The moment we need something, God provides it. He's already prepared for you today what you will need ten years from now. For example, long before Zacchaeus needed to see Jesus, God planted a sycamore tree in Jericho.

Ahasuerus set many goals for launching his Greco-Persian wars. Attaining victory would require financial and military clout, so the king used this six-month-long party to garner financial backing, form vital alliances, and strategize.

Sadly, the text reveals that none of the king's goals included glorifying God. Fill in the blanks from Esther 1:4:

> While he showed the riches of _____
> royal glory and the splendor and pomp of _____
> greatness for many days, 180 days.

Rather than lifting high his God-given blessings for God's glory, Ahasuerus accumulated them for his own selfish gain. Rather than reflecting the glory to God, he absorbed the reverence for himself. Those are spiritually deadly waters to tread, friends.

What is due to God in the following verses?

1 Chronicles 29:11

Psalm 96:6

Psalm 145:5

Only God deserves majesty, glory, and reverence. Everything we have, every blessing we receive, anything admirable that people see in us—it all comes from God. We have anything only because He gave everything.

What do you have in your life right now because of God's goodness to you?

I don't know about you, but I could fill pages. Yes, material things would make the list, but more important are the intangibles, such as love, friendships, and fur babies. Well, fur babies are tangible, but they bring such joy! We have *everything* only because God gave out of His love.

Selfish gain is a spiritually dangerous motivation for any goal. Receiving blessings from God provides us with opportunities to help others, not to fill our storehouses like hoarders.

What does Matthew 6:1–4 say?

Just a few verses later in Matthew 6:19–20, what does Jesus tell us about treasures?

Matthew 6:21 drives home this point with unwavering clarity. Write it out here:

Our story will never end well when the buck stops with us. Ahasuerus centered his efforts on acquiring money, people, and power for himself. The only reason he threw the banquet was to acquire even more.

Two years ago, I downsized from a four-bedroom suburban home to a one-bedroom country cottage surrounded by more trees than neighbors. My home is barely 1,100 square feet, but it is all the space I need, plus some. The back deck is twice the size of my bedroom. My sisters helped build raised garden beds so I could grow fresh vegetables, which I absolutely cherish! God lovingly used downsizing to teach me the blessing of contentment.

Downsizing proved to be one of the most liberating experiences of my life. I feel so *unencumbered*. There is nothing wrong with earthly possessions as long as they don't possess you.

Empire-building took center stage in Ahasuerus's life. What sits at the center of yours?

Ahasuerus centered his life on himself.

In Christ, we have a heavenly King who centered His life around us.

His worldly possessions could fit in a knapsack.

His success was measured in souls gained for heaven.

His joy centered on His relationship with the Father.

His goal was to love us to salvation.

He *gave*.

Long before we knew we needed a Savior, God placed a holy seed in Mary's womb.

Esther was going to marry Ahasuerus—an earthly king of kings and lord of lords. In Jesus Christ, we have the eternal King of kings and Lord of lords. Esther was marrying a selfish man; we are marrying a King who sacrificed Himself to death for us.

The lavish banquet that awaits us in heaven will make Ahasuerus's banquet look like a young girl's playroom teatime. And God woos us not with possessions but with a person—Jesus Christ, our Savior.

That is one banquet we do not want to miss.

DAY 3
Banquets and Persian Opulence

And when these days were completed, the king gave for all the people present in Susa the citadel, both great and small, a feast lasting for seven days in the court of the garden of the king's palace. There were white cotton curtains and violet hangings fastened with cords of fine linen and purple to silver rods and marble pillars, and also couches of gold and silver on a mosaic pavement of porphyry, marble, mother-of-pearl, and precious stones. Drinks were served in golden vessels, vessels of different kinds, and the royal wine was lavished according to the bounty of the king. And drinking was according to this edict: "There is no compulsion." For the king had given orders to all the staff of his palace to do as each man desired.

(Esther 1:5–8)

The empty plates and wine goblets were barely dry from the king's 180-day banquet before his servants pulled them out for yet another party. Apparently, the only difference was the guest list.

Read Esther 1:5–8.

According to Esther 1:5, how long was this second banquet?

Who was invited?

How does this guest list compare with the one in Esther 1:3?

This second banquet was thrown for the common people. After all, their taxes had likely financed the king's first 180-day party. Wouldn't that at least earn them a turkey leg or sausage on a stick?

The cinematographer now pans out to reveal the vivid colors and opulent setting of the palace's garden courtyard. Historians have described in great detail the jaw-dropping extravagance of Persian gardens. They were famous places to display wealth, so Persians spent much time and money cultivating masterpiece gardens.

Archaeologists have uncovered complex watering systems, elaborate fountains, and even statues. Some historians report roaming peacocks in affluent Persian gardens. Intricately designed mosaic tile was often used for walkways amidst vibrant tropical plants.

I love spending time in my gardens at home. There are raised vegetable gardens, a rose garden, and flowering lantana bushes that keep blooming even during hot, humid Texas summers. A simple table with an umbrella and four chairs sits on the deck, surrounded by flowers in colorful pots. A firepit in the corner of the yard allows space to enjoy s'mores with family and friends when autumn's chill arrives. It feels like an oasis. But it would be very shabby, indeed, alongside one of those Persian gardens.

Ahasuerus took his garden to a whole 'notha level, though. As king, I suppose that is standard protocol.

How does Esther 1:6 describe the scene?

Only the elaborate descriptions of the tabernacle (Exodus 25–28) and the temple (1 Kings 7; 2 Chronicles 3–4) surpass the vivid detail provided here! Ancient Greek historians recount how the Persians loved to throw swanky banquets in their garden courtyards.

Have you ever experienced such extravagant surroundings? If so, what was the occasion?

Several years ago, one of the law partners for whom I worked graciously invited me to his daughter's wedding. The dress code was formal black tie. Though he was a humble man of God, he had been blessed with significant inherited wealth. He belonged to Houston's most elite clubs and wore monogrammed, custom-made dress shirts under his custom-tailored suit jackets.

The wedding reception took place at the posh Houston Country Club. I donned my fanciest long dress, slipped on high heels, and nervously walked in. I had never felt so out of place in my entire life. It looked like a Hollywood movie set. Chefs prepared sumptuous food at individual cooking stations, caviar- and brie-laden appetizer tables sat along the gilt mirrored walls, and the finest champagne flowed freely from a fountain. *Literally.* I remember glancing out of the massive cathedral-shaped windows only to see men playing polo on glistening horses as the sun set over a velvety green lawn. It was surreal.

Are you easily swayed or influenced by opulent surroundings?

I was certainly swayed that night. I was young and unmarried at the time, so some small part of me just knew it was the perfect setting for a Prince Charming scenario. I know—silly, right? Alas, it was not meant to be. I wore both of my glass slippers home that evening, but it was nice to dream of being Cinderella for a night.

As fancy as that wedding reception was, I imagine that it still did not hold a candle to what Ahasuerus's working-class guests must have experienced during that seven-day banquet. Speaking of champagne fountains, drinking was encouraged at the king's banquet. A lot of drinking.

According to Esther 1:7, how were the drinks served?

What was the edict regarding drinking in Esther 1:8?

"There is no compulsion." Historians have noted that the decorum for such lavish banquets dictated that when the king drank, everyone drank. Otherwise, a guest was not allowed to drink. However, Ahasuerus dismissed protocol and instituted an open bar to allow guests to drink as much and as often as they wished. After all, he was trying to persuade them to support his wars. Nothing persuades like an excess of alcohol.

Can you imagine the shenanigans in play after a seven-day open bar?

This quote sums it up perfectly: "When inhibitions associated with social conventions disappear in the alcohol vapor, many drinkers allow themselves to violate clear social rules."[7]

Between these two banquets, Ahasuerus displayed an amazing spectacle of royal wealth and extravagance. However, such tendency to show off was not unique to Ahasuerus.

Read Isaiah 39:1–7.

Who was flaunting his wealth and to whom?

In verse 6, what did Isaiah say would happen?

Hezekiah had just revealed the loot that his enemy would soon plunder. It was like showing a jewel thief the combination to your safe and the size of your diamonds. Worldly treasures can be lost in a moment. Just ask anyone who invests in the stock market. We can enjoy the finer things that God provides in this life—He provides them for our delight! However, He does not provide them to define us or to hoard them without sharing.

Read 1 Timothy 6:6–10.

What is the overarching message?

Contentment. We can be content in Christ apart from worldly treasures. The key is faith-filled contentment. It took many years and conquering a mass of debt before I finally learned to find contentment in Christ alone.

What is the difference between happiness and contentment?

Happiness finds its joy in goods; contentment finds its joy in God. If something happens to our goods, happiness hops the next train to Tibet. Nothing can rob our contentment when it is based on Christ alone. God faithfully provides us with our daily necessities (1 Timothy 6:8), so we never have to worry about tomorrow. We may *want* to worry about tomorrow, but we don't *need* to. That's a huge difference.

What does Matthew 6:33 say are our best gifts?

Seeking God first is key. Extravagant materialism does not serve well any believer who wishes to live in holy contentment. How do you practice godly contentment each day?

Practicing godly contentment starts with gratitude. The king's guests were enjoying a glimpse of a lifestyle that was likely very different from their everyday reality. Perhaps like my fairytale experience at that luxurious wedding, the guests simply attended for a short time and returned to life as usual. Ahasuerus's guests were experiencing a paradise of sorts.

Golden goblets with unlimited refills can never fill us with contentment. Only a vibrant, committed, and surrendered life to Jesus Christ allows us to look past life's manicured gardens to see heaven's Master Gardener. When Christ returns and brings us as His Bride to God's lavish wedding feast in heaven, it will far surpass any Cinderella moment we could ever experience on earth.

Esther was an orphan + asks where do we put our focus?

DAY 4
Queen Vashti: The Choice Women Face

Queen Vashti also gave a feast for the women in the palace
that belonged to King Ahasuerus. On the seventh day,
when the heart of the king was merry with wine, he commanded Mehuman, Biztha, Harbona, Bigtha and Abagtha,
Zethar and Carkas, the seven eunuchs who served in the
presence of King Ahasuerus, to bring Queen Vashti before
the king with her royal crown, in order to show the peoples and the princes her beauty, for she was lovely to look
at. But Queen Vashti refused to come at the king's command delivered by the eunuchs. At this the king became
enraged, and his anger burned within him.

(Esther 1:9–12)

For six months plus seven days, Ahasuerus's banquets have taken center
stage. Feasting, drinking, and merriment are in full swing. As our garden
courtyard drama escalates, Persia's Queen Vashti makes her first appearance in the narrative.

Read Esther 1:9–12.

How is Vashti described in verse 11?

The name *Vashti* means "best." Amidst all the lavish surroundings with
her husband as the most powerful man in the civilized world, would we
expect any less? In Herodotus's writings, the Persian queen was named
Amestris. The name Vashti has not been found in any Persian records
to date. However, some scholars believe that Vashti was the queen's
name in Hebrew, while Amestris was her Greek name.

Persian queens were usually wealthy through vast estates and other tangible possessions. Historical writings generally agree that Eastern customs
did not permit women to attend royal feasts or banquets given by the king.

Consequently, what did Vashti do in Esther 1:9?

While the king held his lavish banquet, Queen Vashti hosted one of her own. The "women in the palace" likely referred to the wives of dignitaries attending the king's banquet, along with women from the king's harem.

Even though Ahasuerus was monogamous in marriage, the same cannot be said about his marriage bed. His harem contained more than 360 concubines. Historians have well documented his many affairs, which were regarded as a source of court fascination.

The king's banquet is in full swing, and the party is bubbling along merrily, until his ego takes a hard left into crazy. This rapid-fire emotional change in leaders from happy to furious gives us an interesting glimpse into God's nature. Consider Psalm 2:12: "Kiss the Son, lest He be angry, and you perish in the way, for His wrath is quickly kindled. Blessed are all who take refuge in Him." That same drastic change is implied in the Ten Commandments when God says, "I the Lord your God am a jealous God" (Exodus 20:5). Jealousy is not a carefully calculated, drawn-out change but an extremely quick emotional change.

What did Ahasuerus request in Esther 1:11?

Notice that the text specifically focuses on physical beauty. Ahasuerus was not interested in Vashti's quantum physics skills. Fill in the blanks from Esther 1:11:

> ". . . to bring Queen Vashti before the king with her royal
> _____, in order to _____ the peoples and the princes
> her _____, for she was _____ to _____ at."

Crown. Show. Beauty. Lovely. Look. All exterior references according to the context. Being sized up based on physical attributes summarizes the history of beautiful women. Remember Jacob? He loved beautiful Rachel and hated homely Leah.

Only once in my life did I ever see a woman who was so physically beautiful that I literally stopped and stared. She had long, shiny, jet-black hair, high cheekbones, a perfectly proportioned figure, and porcelain skin. Notably, she wore only the faintest hint of makeup and was casually dressed. I stopped and complimented her. She was an Italian woman in town to visit an American friend. She was pleasantly surprised to receive such a compliment. Incidentally, it was quite refreshing to meet such a naturally beautiful woman who was humble about her appearance.

Have you ever met a woman who was physically stunning? What stood out to you?

Naturally, true beauty comes from the Lord, as we will study later. Vashti was a beautiful woman, but God had also blessed her with a backbone.

When Vashti received the king's summons in Esther 1:11, what did she do in verse 12?

I can almost picture the king's incredulous, openmouthed stare. *Wait, she what?* You could probably hear those poor eunuchs' knees knocking together in fear! I wonder if they did rock-paper-scissors to determine which of them would actually have to articulate Vashti's response to Ahasuerus.

Josephus, another well-known and documented historian, conveyed how harems in some eastern societies were usually sequestered, even riding in closed carriages since the law forbade anyone from gazing on a woman's face in royal charge.

Some scholars have speculated if what Josephus reported was true, then Vashti's impertinence would stem from her objection to being humiliated by appearing in such a public place to be gazed on by the multitudes. And as queen, such an appearance was far beneath her royal station. What woman of substance longs to merely be an ornamental object?

Here, we see the story's first reversal of fortune. Queen Vashti stood firm to guard her dignity and was unceremoniously escorted out of the palace.

What reversals of fortunes have you experienced in your life? How did you handle them?

Reversals of fortune are challenging because we often don't see them coming. Just keep reminding yourself that no reversal surprises God. He already has the perfect plan to guide us, provide exactly what we need, and wipe our tears along the way.

Given the context of the king's party atmosphere, how would you as a woman interpret such a request had you received it?

Some have assumed that Ahasuerus's request insinuated that Vashti appear before the assembly wearing only her royal crown. We do not know if there was anything immodest undergirding the king's request. Whether you agree with Vashti's refusal to degrade herself or object to her refusal to submit to her husband, God does not reveal the specific reason.

When Vashti refused to appear before the king, she committed a triple transgression: a woman who challenged the authority of a man, a wife who disobeyed her husband, and a royal subject who refused to follow a royal command.

In Esther 1:12, what was the king's response to Queen Vashti's refusal?

It is one thing to be humiliated one-on-one, but Ahasuerus endured humiliation before an entire assembly. It was a glaring, public slap in the face.

If the king were to overlook such action, the repercussions could damage his royal and political authority.

The king became enraged, and his anger burned within him.

Those are foreboding words. As we walk through the Book of Esther, it becomes clear that Ahasuerus could control everything but himself. It is helpful to remember that burning anger does not always mean someone who lacks self-control. Each of our sins causes God's fury to flare against us—yet Christ intercedes with His nail-scarred hands. Jesus also exhibited anger and zeal when He cleansed the temple. We can learn something about God as our King from studying Ahasuerus. Thankfully, there are great differences.

Ahasuerus's advisers easily manipulated him; he made rash decisions that he later lamented; and he became furious when his plans veered off course. He built a vast capital city in Susa but failed to build his own character. And he failed to properly build his own marriage.

What does Proverbs 16:32 say about anger?

What does Proverbs 25:28 say about self-control?

God is slow to act on His anger (Psalm 2). His mercy and grace holds that fiery anger in check. Anger is a volatile emotion that must be handled with kid gloves.[8] Many terrible, rash decisions are made in anger. Have you ever experienced that? What happened?

Ahasuerus's behavior did not reflect the godly attribute of self-control. He was the ruler of an immense empire but not ruler of his own emotions.

His banquets aimed at showing the might of the king and his kingdom, but how would men follow his royal command when his own wife refused his request? As a woman, my sympathy goes out to Vashti. She was truly in a lose-lose situation. Honoring the king's request risked her reputation, while refusing the king's request risked her life.

This is the first instance of God's providence in the Book of Esther. Queen Vashti's refusal was the linchpin that began the chain of events that God leveraged to rescue His people from annihilation.

The bottom line? God was still at work, whether or not King Ahasuerus knew it. What does God control according to Proverbs 21:1?

God's sovereignty knows no bounds. He is master over all of creation and over all hearts of the created—including kings. He is still at work in every life on earth today, whether we know Him or not.

Like a master chess champion, God moves hearts, arranges circum-stances, and pushes etiquette until He ultimately brings about His perfect plan. Despite wealthy, materialistic settings such as the Persian Empire, or the most intimate setting such as a human heart, God's flawless plan will never be thwarted.

Even though we tend to judge people by looking at their exterior, the Lord looks at our heart. When the King of kings call us to Him, it is not to walk a runway holding a crown. It is to walk in His ways holding the crown of life.

Thank You, Jesus!

DAY 5
Manipulating Weak Leaders

Then the king said to the wise men who knew the times
(for this was the king's procedure toward all who were
versed in law and judgment. . . .) "According to the law,
what is to be done to Queen Vashti, because she has not
performed the command of King Ahasuerus delivered by
the eunuchs?" . . . "If it please the king, let a royal order go
out from him, and let it be written among the laws of the
Persians and the Medes so that it may not be repealed, that
Vashti is never again to come before King Ahasuerus. And
let the king give her royal position to another who is better
than she."

(Esther 1:13, 15, 19)

As we wrap up Lesson 1, the saga's drama continues. We left off yesterday's lesson on a cliffhanger of impending doom: "The king became enraged, and his anger burned within him." We pick up today as the camera
pans away from the banquet and zooms in on Ahasuerus and his wise men
huddled together trying to figure out the next move in this socially awk-
ward situation.

Read Esther 1:13–22.

How are the wise men described in verse 13?

The Greek historian Herodotus stated that Persian kings surrounded
themselves with a panel of judges (or wise men) on whom the king relied
for accurate interpretations of the law. In that context, the presence of those
particular seven men takes on a whole new meaning, doesn't it?

Apart from their names, how are they identified in Esther 1:14?

Not only were they noblemen (princes), but those men were also experts in the laws of the Medes and Persians. These royal advisers were also political experts, like a presidential candidate's campaign manager. They knew the laws and how to navigate rough political seas.

The Book of Daniel also mentions the laws of the Medes and Persians. What does Daniel 6:15 say about these laws?

In other words, whatever the king decreed was irrevocable, even if he changed his mind later. Significantly, Herodotus also documented that Persian officials made a habit of deciding key issues while intoxicated that they would then confirm once sober. Let that sink in for a moment.

What trouble do you think could happen when important government decisions are made while decision makers are drunk?

Let's just say that less-than-stellar choices can be made while under the influence. In verse 15, what does Ahasuerus ask his wise men?

The king's response was based on the law, not on love. Ahasuerus did not ask the wise men to arrange a private meeting between him and Vashti to resolve their differences. He did not send a note of apology. Women in those days did not have a voice, a point underscored here by Ahasuerus's lack of communication with his wife. Laws are important, but not when it comes to resolving conflict and softening hearts. Perhaps the king was not anxious to discover the reason behind her refusal. Perhaps heart-to-heart talks were not his forte. Whatever his reasoning, he let the law lead rather than relationship.

Regarding Law, what did Christ accomplish according to Matthew 5:17–18?

Jesus came to fulfill all that was written in the Law and the Prophets, and He kept every letter of it perfectly. At Calvary, God poured out His full wrath for our sin penalty on Christ. Christ, not the Law, is the path to righteousness. We have the privilege of looking to Him and Him alone to make us right before God. Christ is the end of the Law for everyone who believes (Romans 10:4).

After listing them by name in verse 14, what do the wise men see?

Why would the author include such a strange phrase as they "saw the king's face"? The words indicate closeness. They were not far-off spectators as Ahasuerus waved from a balcony or gilded throne. Ahasuerus allowed these men into his intimate inner circle as trusted advisers. At such close range, emotions, especially rage and anger, are difficult to mask. The measured tones of the king's anger reverberated from each royal whisker. This "mighty man" was not getting his way—a situation with which the king was not acquainted. Do you sense a royal temper tantrum forthcoming?

In Esther 1:16, how does Memucan classify Vashti's actions?

He adds fuel to the fire by classifying Vashti's actions as a melodramatic, kingdomwide debacle. There is much to applaud about advisers who keep their cool when situations heat up. Clearly, Memucan is not such an adviser.

In verses 17–18, how does Memucan believe the queen's behavior will influence Persia's women?

Oh, the *drama*. Memucan's exaggeration assumes that all women will begin emulating Vashti's impertinence, thereby causing a kingdomwide feminist revolt. But hold on to your wigs. Here comes the best part.

In verses 19–20, what is Memucan's advice to Ahasuerus?

His advice is threefold: (1) dismiss Vashti, (2) find another queen, and (3) issue a royal decree that Persian women should honor their husbands. Basically, get rid of her, replace her, and remind all women of their submissive, voiceless role. *Ouch.*

Do you find Memucan's recommendations to be sound? Why or why not?

Perhaps because I am a woman, I find his recommendation and proposed course of action wholly ridiculous and—might I add—just a *tad* egotistical. If you received a presidential executive order to honor, respect, and love your husband more, would it work? I don't think so. Those qualities of honor, respect, and love cannot be produced on demand. A piece of paper is a poor substitute for proper relational intimacy.

But let's not point every finger at Ahasuerus. Scripture does not record that Vashti tried to communicate with her husband, either. No request from the queen trying to explain her response or note requesting a private conversation was rejected by the king, because perhaps they were never sent. It takes two to tango.

In relying on the law and not on personal relationship, on melodramatic advice instead of on private conversation, God used Ahasuerus's communication failure to open a vacancy in the queen's office for the one He will use to save His people. A vital plot development!

In Esther 1:19, what kind of law does Memucan reference?

As we glimpsed earlier in the study, it was believed that the law of the Medes and Persians could not be repealed according to one of Hammurabi's laws. The legendary Code of Hammurabi originated from a Babylonian ruler named Hammurabi, who lived from 1810 to 1750 BC. He authored 282 laws (or series of enactments) to govern polite society on various subjects, including marriage, slavery, and inheritance

Some of Hammurabi's laws are still used today. In fact, a reproduction of a portion of the Code of Hammurabi hangs in the building of the United States Supreme Court. The actual 7.5-foot original carving of the Code of Hammurabi stands preserved in the Louvre in Paris, France.

One of the laws contained in the Code of Hammurabi states that no judge could change a royal decree. Some historians believe that the laws of the Medes and Persians mimicked those parameters. Greek historical resources are conflicted. Either way, Ahasuerus's wise men relied on those laws as an authoritative force in making their decisions.

What does Romans 13:1–2 say about authority?

God alone holds ultimate authority over all. He has placed governing authorities over us to follow the laws of the land. When people are given a position of authority, it is imperative to remember that their authority is God-given, not self-earned. Leaders who allow pride and ego to interfere in decision-making discover that submitting to God can be a hard lesson to learn.

Every man or woman occupying a position of authority is second-in-command under Jesus Christ, who is Lord of all. Neither Ahasuerus nor his wise men were exempt.

By following the unwise suggestion of his wise men, King Ahasuerus publicized his lack of authority and embarrassment that he could not rule over his own household. And to expedite the embarrassment, he distributed the decree in a lickety-split manner through the original Pony Express. No, it wasn't actually called the Pony Express, but among its many accomplishments, the Persian Empire was known for its effective communication system. Rather than technology, they relied on men and horses.

In today's technological superhighway, we are accustomed to instant communication. We can connect instantaneously with someone on the other side of world.

In just the past few days, what means of instant communication have you used?

So Ahasuerus's self-serving decree was disseminated across the entire Persian Empire. According to Esther 1:22, how was the decree written?

Language barriers would offer no excuse for not following the king's decree. As each household received the news, we can only assume how those words were viewed—by husbands and wives alike.

What we never see is how Vashti reacted to being dismissed. Her bags were immediately packed, and she never exchanged another word with her husband. I wonder what she would have thought about her ex-husband's post-dismissal decree.

A study note in *The Lutheran Study Bible* for Esther 1:19 provides a helpful insight about the important role that Vashti later played in the kingdom of Persia:

> The king took this advice and dismissed his defiant wife from attending him; a divorce was decreed. Vashti was not killed; she reappears in historical documents as a powerful adviser to her son Artaxerxes until her death in 424 BC.

As we reach the end of the first chapter of Esther, what three things most stand out to you? Why?

1.

2.

3.

Lavish banquets, opulent surroundings, and court intrigue sit fresh in our minds. We met the Persian Empire's drama king and queen. We will not see Vashti again in the story, but Ahasuerus's difficulties are only just beginning.

In our next lesson, we look forward to meeting our story's heroine and hero. I don't know about you, but this story already reads like a blockbuster movie script!

Before you close the book, would you spend some time in prayer? His Word is life and has the power to transform you from the inside out. Ask God to grow your faith and spiritually strengthen you for the road ahead. If you struggle with being treated as a trophy instead of a daughter of the King, ask God for His wisdom.

Even though the Book of Esther tells a compelling story, none is more compelling than God sending His Son to nail your sin to the cross. Keep studying and walking! You are in my prayers with each step.

LESSON 2

Stepping Up past Fear

Esther 2

As Esther was chosen to replace the deposed Queen Vashti, life as she knew it would never again be the same. Esther had no choice but to play their game. Women, especially a foreigner in a foreign land, had no power or voice. Esther followed her cousin's advice to hide her Jewish identity and enter the king's harem. After submitting to a year of beauty treatments, she spent one night with the king. By God's perfect providence, Esther won the heart of the king and was crowned queen of Persia. But she would soon learn that the opulent beauty of the palace was a deadly facade.

- DAY 1   The Miss Persia Contest *(Esther 2:1–4)*
- DAY 2   Mordecai the Jew *(Esther 2:5–7)*
- DAY 3   Inside the King's Harem *(Esther 2:8–11)*
- DAY 4   Hail, Queen Esther! *(Esther 2:12–18)*
- DAY 5   Unrewarded Loyalty *(Esther 2:19–23)*

KEY QUESTIONS

- Do you make moral judgments about the actions of others, whether or not you know all the facts?
- When was the last time you faced a difficult ethical dilemma?
- Did others judge your resulting decision or actions?

DAY 1
The Miss Persia Contest

After these things, when the anger of King Ahasuerus had abated, he remembered Vashti and what she had done and what had been decreed against her. Then the king's young men who attended him said, "Let beautiful young virgins be sought out for the king. And let the king appoint officers in all the provinces of his kingdom to gather all the beautiful young virgins to the harem in Susa the citadel, under custody of Hegai, the king's eunuch, who is in charge of the women. Let their cosmetics be given them. And let the young woman who pleases the king be queen instead of Vashti." This pleased the king, and he did so.

(Esther 2:1–4)

In an effort to attract post-summer business to Atlantic City in the summer of 1921, local businessmen joined forces and invited bathing suit–clad young women to compete for the title of most beautiful woman. It was a resounding success, and the Miss America pageant was born that day. A century later, it continues as the longest-running beauty contest in the world.

That first contest contained no talent competition or intellectual question segment. Women were judged strictly on physical beauty. The first young lady who was crowned Miss America was a sixteen-year-old high school junior from Washington. Years later, she admitted in an interview that she wished she had never been part of the contest. As age faded her physical beauty, people compared her to her sixteen-year-old pictures and judged her worth accordingly.

The criteria used in the first Miss America contest fit the criteria used in King Ahasuerus's Miss Persia contest like a form-fitting ballgown.

Read Esther 2:1–4.

What are the first three words of Esther 2:1?

After what things? Nearly four years have passed since the king dismissed Vashti. Ahasuerus's opulent banquets provided the various levels of support that he needed to wage his war against Greece. His two ill-fated military campaigns were miserable failures, and the king returned home in humiliation. Now he's back home licking his wounds and trying to figure out how to replenish his drained treasuries.

In Esther 2:1, what did the king remember after his anger had abated?

When the king returns home with his tail between his legs, he remembers that he has no queen to greet him. Perhaps he began to regret his anger-driven decision to dismiss Vashti. Maybe he missed her. Perhaps he felt more vulnerable without her by his side. The Hebrew word for "remembered" (זכר, *zakar)* used here occurs other times in the Old Testament.

It is often used when God *remembers* something or someone with concern and empathy. What did God *zakar* in the following verses?

Genesis 8:1

Genesis 9:15–16

Genesis 19:28–29

God's *remembering* is often connected to His covenant promises. Ahasuerus cannot claim such a noble sentiment. Ahasuerus possessed hundreds of concubines, but that one special person was absent. Perhaps in this moment, Ahasuerus learned the difference between love and sex, between a life partner and a superficial ornament. Loneliness echoes loud in the dark of night. The text does not reveal the king's feelings, but it is telling that the Miss Persia contest began soon after his return from his failed Greco-Persian wars.

What do the young men suggest to Ahasuerus in Esther 2:2?

You can almost hear the cattle wrangler shouting, "Okay, boys, bring in the herd!" (Well, maybe that's because I'm a Texan.) It comes as no surprise that the king's advisers were eager to quickly replace Vashti since they had suggested her removal. After all, a lonely king could become a vengeful king.

According to Esther 2:3, what do they suggest as the process for selecting a new queen?

Choosing such a public avenue to choose a royal wife was rare. In Scripture, we do not read that Solomon, David, or any other ruler conducted such a wife-seeking spectacle. Their royal wives were usually chosen based on their lineage or political alliance.

Once again, Ahasuerus puts his self-interests above his empire. He didn't even take time to set search parameters for his advisers to follow. A politically advantageous marriage could have provided kingdomwide benefits and even financial benefits. Ahasuerus's lack of guidelines reveals his lack of leadership.

Historians have uncovered only one documented occurrence of such a "beauty search." In about AD 600, the Sasanian king Chosroes II commanded his kingdom's satraps to seek out beautiful girls to be presented to him as new-queen material. Other kings sought political marriages to secure their borders. King Solomon used that strategy to bring about unprecedented peace during his reign.

Interestingly, in Eswatini (formerly known as Swaziland) in Southern Africa, the reigning king still chooses a new bride each year from thousands of virgins. *Each year.* This polygamous king, along with the entire village, watches the virgins perform a seminude ritual dance while waving a tall cane (symbolizing their virginity) in hopes of being chosen.

For a woman, those examples are hard to swallow. Thankfully, Scripture provides us with an encouraging example of how a godly man searches for a wife.

Read Genesis 24:1–14.

Abraham desired a kindred wife for his son. He never mentioned beauty, not even once. He also instructed his servant to leave behind any woman who was unwilling to leave her land. In other words, leave behind any woman who was unwilling to leave her father and mother to become one flesh with her husband.

When the servant arrived in Nahor, he prayed that God would reveal to him a generous, kind woman with a servant heart.

Whom did God provide in verses 15–20, and what attributes did she possess?

Not only did God meet all of Abraham's and his servant's requests, but He went above and beyond. God *immediately* provided a young, beautiful virgin with kindred ties and a kind heart.

How does Isaac's search for a wife compare to Ahasuerus's search?

Which search would you prefer to be a part of?

When we long to honor God with our choice of a spouse, God will often far exceed our expectations! I have heard many women express how weary they are of waiting for God to provide a godly husband. Even though God provided Rebekah immediately for Isaac, remember that Isaac was approximately forty years old at the time. He was more than twice the normal marrying age. Our *immediately* is not the same as God's *immediately*. We take hope from the fact that God's perfect plan contains no statute of limitations.

In stark contrast, describe what kind of women were sought by Ahasuerus in Esther 2:3 and the extent of the search.

Ahasuerus's kingdomwide search was based on physical appearance and virgin status. There's no mention of seeking out a great conversationalist, a woman with a sense of humor, kindness, or even intelligence.

What does that reveal about the king's desires?

First-century historian Josephus estimated that there were roughly twenty-five million people in the Persian Empire at that time, including several million women. We do not know how long the king's beauty search lasted, but Josephus noted that the initial screening criteria narrowed likely candidates down to around four hundred women.

In Esther 2:3, what happened to the women who were chosen in round 1?

Let's pause a moment. Not a spa *day,* but a spa *year.* The women chosen were not candidates for an ugly-duckling-to-swan makeover. They were *already* young and lovely. This mindset saturates our culture today. Women endure a never-ending stream of beauty treatments, cosmetic procedures, and other routines to make them more physically attractive, because to some, already being young and lovely is not enough.

What does God say about beauty in the following passages?

1 Samuel 16:7

Proverbs 11:22

Proverbs 31:30

In your own words, what do you think it means to be beautiful in God's eyes?

Time fades physical beauty—it's just a disheartening fact of life. Why put all of our energy and resources into preserving something that has a 100 percent chance of deteriorating?

Ahasuerus's wife-search criteria never penetrated beyond skin deep. Thankfully, your heavenly King is concerned about your heart, not your hair. Your faith, not your figure. Yes, physical beauty can be used to glorify God, but physical beauty is not a prerequisite to a God-fulfilled, joyful life.

On earth, we will never achieve perfection, physically or otherwise, because true beauty is in the eyes of the heart. God desires that we become more like His Son. And such spiritual beauty penetrates to our very soul.

Any time and resources that you invest in learning the Word of God has a 100 percent chance of transforming you into the likeness of Jesus. And, ladies, there is nothing more beautiful than that!

DAY 2
Mordecai the Jew

Now there was a Jew in Susa the citadel whose name was
Mordecai, the son of Jair, son of Shimei, son of Kish, a
Benjaminite, who had been carried away from Jerusalem among the captives carried away with Jeconiah king
of Judah, whom Nebuchadnezzar king of Babylon had
carried away. He was bringing up Hadassah, that is Esther,
the daughter of his uncle, for she had neither father nor
mother. The young woman had a beautiful figure and was
lovely to look at, and when her father and her mother died,
Mordecai took her as his own daughter.

(Esther 2:5–7)

Like a sunbeam breaking through dark storm clouds, here we finally
glimpse a shining ray of hope into a materialistic, overindulgent nation.
Until now, our story has revolved around power struggles, gluttony, god-
lessness, drunkenness, anger, and melodrama. Enter from stage right our
hero and heroine.

Read Esther 2:5–7.

List everything that the text reveals about Mordecai:

The name *Mordecai* is mentioned over fifty times in the Book of Esther,
and he is specifically identified as a Jew on seven occasions—the first being
right here in Esther 2:5. After Cyrus's decree, the freed Judahites started
to be identified as Jews. Even though many returned to the land God had
given their forefathers, some of the Jews decided to remain in the land of
their captivity for reasons not revealed in the text. This lineage is an integral
piece of the puzzle to our story, so highlight this for easy reference later.

Mordecai does not enter the storyline alone. Mordecai's ancestors chose to remain in Persia.

In order to understand the drama that is about to unfold, we need to understand the drama in Mordecai's family tree. Mordecai is identified as a Benjaminite. According to 1 Samuel 9:1 and 9:21, who was Mordecai's distant relation?

Mordecai came from the tribe of Benjamin (Jacob's youngest son [Genesis 35:22–26]), one of Israel's twelve tribes. Kish was a Benjaminite and had a son named Saul. God anointed Saul as the first king of Israel. Consequently, Mordecai belonged to the same tribe and shared the same lineage with King Saul.

If you have ever spent time uncovering your family tree, chances are you discovered interesting, if not surprising, facts. Mordecai was an Israelite to the core with a long, illustrious lineage dating back several generations, spanning several hundred years.

Mordecai is also a Jew, part of God's chosen people.

Reread Esther 2:7.

List everything that the text reveals about Esther:

Esther was a lovely Israelite (Judean) young woman who had been taken in by her cousin Mordecai after her parents' deaths. The name *Esther* originates from the Persian word meaning "star" and also from Ishtar, the Babylonian goddess of love.

However, Esther was born with the Hebrew name *Hadassah*, which means "myrtle." Significantly, myrtle is fragrant when crushed. When Jesus was crushed for our iniquities (Isaiah 53:5), the fragrance of God's love, grace, and hope of salvation filled the earth.

Much like today, orphans have little, if any, control over their lives. Thankfully, after Esther's parents died, her older cousin Mordecai welcomed her into his home as an adopted daughter.

What comes to mind when you hear the word *adopted*?

Adoption is a legal action through which an adult takes into his family a child not his own. It is a loving choice to confer on that child all of the rights and privileges of a natural-born child. Mordecai was already family, yet he chose to step up to the plate and include Esther in his home.

By the sheer grace and love of God, He has adopted you as a daughter. You have been chosen. What do the following verses say about being adopted into His family?

Romans 8:14–17

Galatians 3:25–29

Through Jesus Christ, you and I have been adopted into God's eternal family. When you are adopted into His family through Baptism, you are granted all of the rights and privileges of His children. Through the blood of our Lord and Savior, Jesus Christ, God invites us to draw near to Him with a sincere heart and full assurance of faith. Through His death and resurrection, He conferred on us the right to call God *Father*. He is your strong Father who takes you in and defends you against life's bullies.

Mordecai adopted Esther, who now quietly takes her place onstage to bring faith, courage, dutiful obedience, excellent manners, grace, and intelligence to the big screen. In Mordecai and Esther, we see the hope of God slip in under the radar of a pagan world.

Ironically, had Vashti not taken a stand and been rudely yanked off-stage, Esther would have never been part of the story. Another example of God's faithful providence in action!

How would you define God's providence in your own words?

Simply stated: Providence is God's concentration focused everywhere. No nuance in life, whether large or small, escapes His divine gaze or watchful care. Providence comes from the two-part Latin word *provide*. *Pro* means "on behalf of," and *vide* means "to see." God sees what we need and provides it on our behalf in accordance with His perfect will.

Time and again throughout this study, we will see God's providence—not in the shadows, but lit up center stage. Scene by scene and day by day, God uses the faithful obedience of Esther to save a nation from genocide.

Keep on studying, sister! God still has so much to show us.

DAY 3
Inside the King's Harem

> So when the king's order and his edict were proclaimed, and when many young women were gathered in Susa the citadel in custody of Hegai, Esther also was taken into the king's palace and put in custody of Hegai, who had charge of the women. And the young woman pleased him and won his favor. And he quickly provided her with her cosmetics and her portion of food, and with seven chosen young women from the king's palace, and advanced her and her young women to the best place in the harem. Esther had not made known her people or kindred, for Mordecai had commanded her not to make it known. And every day Mordecai walked in front of the court of the harem to learn how Esther was and what was happening to her.
>
> (Esther 2:8–11)

Today's lesson is a scene in motion. The Miss Persia contest is in full swing, and our heroine has appeared for the first time. Let's start today by remembering (again) how the author describes Esther.

Reread Esther 2:7.

The one Judean who would need to be the most attractive to King Ahasuerus just happened to be a knockout. Do you sense that God is up to something? Me too.

Read Esther 2:8–11.

The author wastes no words describing how Esther felt. She was merely a faceless trophy among many at the mercy of a womanizing, pagan king and his minions. Esther, a young woman without voice or vote, followed instructions without question.

Esther was "taken" into the king's palace and put in the custody of the harem's eunuch. Even though it sounds ominous, "taken" in the Hebrew is a passive form of "to be taken away." It indicates that Esther was not rounded up and escorted into the palace at sword point. She obediently followed when she was chosen.

Esther finds herself in a setting she likely never imagined. As a former orphan, the whole atmosphere must have felt surreal.

What is the first sentence in Esther 2:9?

The whole situation likely made Esther's skin crawl in revulsion. Esther's submissive behavior exhibited tremendous strength and wisdom to follow authority.

As a result of Esther's obedience, what does Hegai's treatment of Esther reveal in verse 9?

Esther followed Hegai's guidance without arguing the proposed course of treatments or demanding luxuries greater than the other women, and she was rewarded accordingly. Simply put, she was *not* a drama queen.

Drama queens are adult versions of playground mean girls. How do you handle drama queens in your life, if you have any? What is most challenging about a drama queen?

Esther's obedient behavior demonstrated her realization that the invisible hand of God was guiding her circumstances for purposes she could not yet see. So she followed, one step at a time, the path that He illuminated in front of her.

People could have judged Esther's path as grievous sin and complete moral decay. They could have judged how she appeared to blatantly abandoned her lineage and all of the teachings in the Jewish Bible. They could have said that she was doing this for position, wealth, or even sex.

Regardless of what people may have said or thought, Esther kept walking through the doors that God opened. Esther's path would have been hard to swallow for any God-fearing woman.

Have you ever made a moral judgment about the actions of another, whether or not you knew all of the facts? If so, what happened? What was the result?

When was the last time you faced a difficult ethical dilemma? If so, how did you resolve it?

Did others judge your resulting decision or actions?

Did you notice that God did not remove Esther from her challenging circumstances? God was providentially working in Esther's circumstances. Whether or not Esther could see the hand of God moving, His hand was there all along.

When circumstances spin beyond your control, how do you typically respond?

When was the last time you prayed for God to change your circumstances or give you the eyes of faith to see how He was working in them? What happened?

Most of us will try to control our circumstances in our own strength when we cannot discern a solution through the fog. What does Isaiah 45:15 reveal about God?

God is a God who sometimes chooses to remain hidden, but that doesn't mean He has exited stage left from your circumstances. Sometimes, it's hard to know that God sees our struggles yet does not remove us from them. Yet in those struggles, He faithfully strengthens our faith.

When it came time for one of my nephews to learn how to walk, he was not jazzed about it. Each time my sister put him down to walk, he threw a jaw-dropping fit. But because of my sister's great love for him, she endured his tears, knowing that the muscles he was building would strengthen him to walk upright in life. God sees our tears, yet in His great love He desires to build our muscles of faith to face life's circumstances we encounter.

What did Mordecai command Esther in 2:10?

Why would Mordecai warn her against disclosing her lineage?

Esther and Mordecai were foreigners living in a pagan land. Even though they were part of God's chosen people, they learned to blend in to avoid persecution and successfully build a fruitful life. It is certainly not a sin for someone to hide their nationality any more than it's a sin for a woman to hide her gray roots. History has repeatedly taught us that sometimes it is necessary in order to avoid danger. We need only to look back a few generations to Hitler and World War II.

Scripture also confirms that the choice to conceal one's identity was not unusual. In Genesis 12:10–13, who conceals their identity and why?

Concealing Sarai's identity as Abraham's wife eventually allowed them to pass through a land where they could have been taken captive. Yet God still blessed Abraham by preserving him and making his offspring as numerous as the stars. God made Abraham the father of many nations, through whom would come Jesus Christ, the promised Savior of the world.

God still blessed the Benjaminites Esther and Mordecai by preserving the lineage of Christ that was carried in the tribe of Judah. Because Esther was born into the Jewish race, God used her unique lineage and position to save His chosen people from slaughter.

Up to this point in the story, Esther has yet to utter a single word. And boy that is *hard* for a woman! Esther excelled at listening. She heard the advice of older, wiser Mordecai and followed it without question. Esther listened to Mordecai's wise instructions much like Ruth listened to Naomi's.

Read Ruth 3:1–13.

After Naomi was left without her two sons and her husband, Ruth, her daughter-in-law, refused to abandon Naomi. Even though Naomi gave Ruth her blessing to leave, Ruth persevered in a strange land to honor Naomi. She faithfully followed Naomi's wise advice, and God blessed her for it.

Write out Ruth 4:13.

Even though Ruth's circumstances played out in the quiet, small Jewish village of Bethlehem, and Esther's played out in the energetic, pagan city of Susa, God was fully present and active in both worlds.

As God guided Ruth to glean stubble in the fields, He guided Esther to win favor in a pagan palace. God is sovereign over the fields in Ruth, and He is sovereign over the feasts in Esther. No one (whether believer or unbeliever) can elude the vigilant eye or faithful hand of God.

Write out Ephesians 1:11.

God works all things according to His will. God *is* working. God is present and active. He never promises to remove us from challenging circumstances:

> God does not promise to raise up every person who suffers in this life as he raised up Esther. But by the example of Esther, He shows us that He is a "father of the fatherless" and a deliverer of the poor and needy. Many poor Jewish girls living in captivity did not attain the kind of royal honor that Esther received. Yet if they called upon God by faith in their distress and looked to the One who promised a Savior to end the world's pain and misery by answering for its cause, then they in the end receive a greater deliverance and salvation from God than the one enjoyed by Esther as queen of Persia.[9]

Like Esther, when you commit to leveraging any influence that God has given you in your home, community, church, or workplace—in whatever circumstances He places you—there is no limit to what God can accomplish through you.

DAY 4
Hail, Queen Esther!

When the turn came for Esther the daughter of Abihail the uncle of Mordecai, who had taken her as his own daughter, to go in to the king, she asked for nothing except what Hegai the king's eunuch, who had charge of the women, advised. Now Esther was winning favor in the eyes of all who saw her. And when Esther was taken to King Ahasuerus, into his royal palace, in the tenth month, which is the month of Tebeth, in the seventh year of his reign, the king loved Esther more than all the women, and she won grace and favor in his sight more than all the virgins, so that he set the royal crown on her head and made her queen instead of Vashti. Then the king gave a great feast for all his officials and servants; it was Esther's feast. He also granted a remission of taxes to the provinces and gave gifts with royal generosity.

(Esther 2:15–18)

Several years ago, I was asked to lead Bible studies on two Christian cruises to the Western Caribbean. As a thank-you, one of the ladies in our group gifted me and my best friend with an onboard spa package of three onboard treatments for each of us. Now I have a confession: I am *extraordinarily* ticklish. With that being said, I do not usually gravitate to spa days. However, she would not allow me to turn down her generous gift. So I thanked her and set the appointment.

On the appointed sea day, we changed into the luxurious, fluffy white robes and matching slippers to enjoy an afternoon of relaxed pampering. One of the services they offered was a hot oil scalp massage. *I did not know that such a thing was even a thing, y'all.* Once they finished my hand massage and manicure, it was time for the oil scalp massage. They recommended saving it for last because they assured us that it was so relaxing we would want to nap afterward.

They settled me into a plush, overstuffed chair and reclined my head back over a basin. Then the lady began gently kneading warm, scented oil all over my scalp. It was so relaxing that I even dozed off at one point. When she returned my chair upright several minutes later, my friend looked over and immediately burst out laughing. When I looked in the mirror I saw why. My oil-saturated hair was sticking straight up in all directions like an Edward Scissorhands session gone amok.

That afternoon spa day felt delightful. It was a rare treat that I have yet to repeat. The next morning, I felt rejuvenated and ready to hike Dunn's River Falls in Jamaica.

In the Book of Esther, Esther and the four hundred women chosen in Ahasuerus's Miss Persia contest were about to undergo twelve months of spa treatments. After my onboard experience, I can't help but think that those women probably longed for sleep 24/7 due to the sheer relaxation factor. Let's put on our fluffy robes and slippers as the story continues at the Persian spa.

After Esther was chosen to be taken into the palace with the other women, what beauty regimen did they experience in Esther 2:12?

I wonder if it was a woman who suggested twelve months of receiving oil, spices, and ointment treatments. Being confined with hundreds of women had to get stressful at times! Because, let's face it, ladies, women can be downright mean sometimes, especially when it comes to beauty and men.

Esther was also given "her portion of food" (Esther 2:9) along with the yearlong beauty treatments. These foods would have promoted good health, along with healthy skin and hair. Although the women may have also received court etiquette training, such instruction was not important enough to make the list.

Stepping Up past Fear

Again, Esther remains silent and follows the beauty treatments as instructed. There are many examples in Scripture of God's people in foreign lands who refused to succumb to pagan rules and practices. Daniel is a perfect example.

Read Daniel 1:8–9.

Even though he was a captive in a foreign land, Daniel remained faithful to God and refused to eat the rich foods prescribed by the king. What was the result in Daniel 1:15?

God gave Daniel favor with the king's eunuchs. It is easy to compare Daniel's situation with that of Esther and call one better than the other. However, God also granted to Esther the favor of the king's eunuchs.

Even though both Daniel and Esther were granted God's favor with the royal eunuchs, their greatest challenges lay ahead. Daniel's future still held a night in the lions' den. Esther's future still held spending one night with the king.

Read Esther 2:12–18.

As a young virgin, Esther must have felt tremors of fear at the prospect of spending the night with Ahasuerus. After all, she had been orphaned at a young age and lived with her older male cousin. As a woman, I pray that God provided a wise, older woman behind the scenes in Esther's life with whom she could talk through such intensely private and sensitive matters before that night arrived.

After each woman spent her appointed night with Ahasuerus, what was the fate of the women who were not chosen as queen in Esther 2:14?

Historians record that being taken into the king's palace was most likely a life sentence. Since the women had been touched by royalty, no other man could touch them. While life in Ahasuerus's harem offered materialistic indulgences, it offered no intimacy of a normal marital relationship. If not chosen as queen, the woman would be relegated to a husbandless existence for the rest of her days. Having the king's child would be their sole consolation. Although the king may offer occasional bedroom visits, he did not offer true companionship. Esther's precarious path was no stroll through the daisy fields.

But God had blessed Esther with brains as well as beauty. What did she do in Esther 2:15?

Unfamiliar with court life, Esther placed herself in the care of someone who was. She had won favor with the harem's head eunuch, so she trusted and followed Hegai's advice. He knew what the king liked. He clothed her accordingly and also instructed her on what to take with her during her evening with Ahasuerus.

Seeking wise counsel and heeding their advice is a vital, godly attribute. What do the following verses teach us about that?

Proverbs 12:15

Proverbs 13:10

Proverbs 15:22

Seeking counsel and advice is wisdom. As Christians, any such advice needs to agree with Scripture. In addition to the Lord, from whom do you seek wise counsel?

The Lord has blessed me with a number of wise, godly friends and mentors. Sometimes, God provides the perfect solution to me by simply talking over a situation with them. Other times, I approach them with specific questions to wrestle through. Honest, open communication and ongoing prayer are key!

A POLITICAL VIEWPOINT

In November 2019, I co-led a pilgrimage tour to the Holy Land. Our Israeli tour guide, Ori Katzir, had previously, for over a decade, worked as an Israeli foreign news correspondent. Over the course of our tour, we talked at length about the Book of Esther since I was in the middle of writing this study.

I wanted to understand Esther from his firsthand cultural perspective. Ori is a Jewish father of two, who raised his children in Jewish tradition. I asked if he would have allowed his daughter to participate in a scenario similar to Esther. He vehemently responded that he would have exercised everything within his power to prevent it.

Although Christian Scripture is silent about Mordecai's precise motivation, Ori suggested that Mordecai held political aspirations. Since I have no background in politics, it was an intriguing hypothesis that I had not even considered. I asked Ori for the basis of his conclusion. He had written a sixty-page scholarly paper on the Book of Esther from a political perspective and forwarded it to me to read. He wrote:

> The Scroll writer does not mention anywhere that Mordecai bothered to hide Esther, sending her to relatives in Judea or anywhere else, or pairing her with a kosher Jew so that she

does not fall victim to the desires of a Gentile king and lover of women.[10]

He elaborates that Mordecai held an unknown position in Ahasuerus's government. What if he had his sights set on becoming prime minister in Haman's place? What better way to monitor the movements and thoughts of the king than to place a spy in the king's bedroom? An interesting perspective, indeed.

When it comes to studying God's Word, asking questions is as important as the source you consult. Ori is a political expert, and I greatly respect his knowledge in that area as I have absolutely zero. As a woman of faith, I cannot remove God or His providential hand from Esther's story. Consequently, our opinions differ regarding Mordecai's and Esther's motivations.

However, my conversations with Ori inspired me to consider a broader scope and really dig into Scripture to discern the truth. Sounds like the Bereans, doesn't it? I pray that you are never hesitant to ask questions, sisters. Hearing differing viewpoints stretches and strengthens our faith muscles as we examine and articulate why we believe what we believe.

Finally, the hour has arrived for Esther to walk the long hall to the king's bedchamber.

What happens according to Esther 2:16–17?

God's hand of providence had faithfully guided Esther to wear a queen's coronet. And God even went a step further: Esther won not only the king's favor, but she also won his heart. You don't win someone's heart with an oil-scented body. A well-coifed exterior is cold without inner warmth and beauty. Esther was a woman of substance beyond physical attributes.

What is God's beauty treatment according to 1 Timothy 2:9–10?

True beauty is not passive—it is active in modesty and good works. Those godly, good works include loving as Christ loved us and relying on the fruit of the Spirit from Galatians 5:22–23 to honor Him with our words and actions. Outward beauty is a facade without the glow of inner beauty. Even Socrates famously said, "Grant that I may become inwardly beautiful."

After undergoing twelve months of beauty treatments and probably feeling more than a little anxiety, Esther emerged wearing the crown as queen of Persia. Perhaps Esther hated her circumstances with all of her heart. Maybe she felt that harem life violated every conviction and moral principle that her long-lost parents and Mordecai had taught her. Possibly she wondered how God could have let such a degrading situation come to pass.

The Apocrypha records this prayer of Esther:

> You have knowledge of all things; and you know that I hate the splendor of the wicked and abhor the bed of the uncircumcised and of any alien. You know my necessity—that I abhor the sign of my proud position, which is upon my head on the days when I appear in public. I abhor it like a menstrual rag, and I do not wear it on the days when I am at leisure. . . . Your servant has had no joy since the day that I was brought here until now, except in you, O Lord God of Abraham.
>
> (Addition C, 14:15–16, 18)[11]

What Scripture confirms is that Esther listened to wise counsel and hid her Jewish identity. Consequently, God's plan to place a royal crown on Esther's head came to pass. She trusted God, and a whole nation would owe her their lives.

Ahasuerus has a new queen! And true to character, he immediately throws a feast to celebrate. What did he do according to Esther 2:18?

What was the feast called?

The king was in love, so his heart overflowed with generosity. And he wanted no ambiguity about whom he desired to honor. Throughout the Book of Esther, banquets and feasts play a significant part in role reversals. During the king's seven-day banquet in Esther 1, Vashti was dismissed as queen. In this feast, Esther is embraced as queen. There was a stark contrast between queens. For Queen Vashti, the king flaunted his wealth and tried to parade his wife. For Queen Esther, the king gave his wealth and honored his wife.

Which queen would you rather be? Why?

So Esther won the affection of the king and a highly sought-after position in the kingdom. By following the wise counsel of Mordecai and Hegai, Esther was now placed by God in a position of influence.

When we faithfully follow God and advice from wise, godly counselors, the blessings are abundant. Even in those blessings, the challenges may be equally abundant.

But God's Word is crystal clear. When we follow His lead, the path leads to life eternal with Jesus Christ, our Savior and King.

DAY 5
Unrewarded Loyalty

In those days, as Mordecai was sitting at the king's gate,
Bigthan and Teresh, two of the king's eunuchs, who guarded the threshold, became angry and sought to lay hands
on King Ahasuerus. And this came to the knowledge of
Mordecai, and he told it to Queen Esther, and Esther told
the king in the name of Mordecai. When the affair was
investigated and found to be so, the men were both hanged
on the gallows. And it was recorded in the book of the
chronicles in the presence of the king.

(Esther 2:21–23)

Archaeological digs in Susa have revealed much about Persian life
during the days of Ahasuerus. Specifically, they unearthed a massive gatehouse approximately one hundred yards from the palace.

The gate's opening is a whopping fifty feet wide. The gatehouse boasts
four towers on the outside, and on the inside are four, forty-foot high deco-
rated pillars through which visitors could access the palace complex. They
identified an inscription at the gate indicating that it was built by Ahasuerus's father, Darius the Great.

A city's gate was the main location for its citizens to conduct business,
air grievances, form important alliances, decide legal matters, receive the
latest news, socialize, and much more.

In each of the following verses, what takes place at the city gate?

Genesis 19:1

Deuteronomy 21:18–19

Ruth 4:1–12

1 Samuel 4:16–18

So why all of this information about a gate? While Esther was secluded in the king's palace, Mordecai could not look after her as he did before, so he placed himself at the center of the action—the city gate.

Read Esther 2:19–23.

Where was Mordecai sitting?

Can you imagine the level of concern and worry that Mordecai experienced? His young cousin, whom he had taken in after her parents died and had raised like a daughter, was beyond his protection. After all, he was the one who asked Esther to keep their family background secret.

Imagine his self-dialogue and the questions that haunted him: *Has she kept the secret? If not, is she being punished for concealing her lineage? How is she doing? Is she making friends? Does she have all that she needs? Does the king really love her? Is anyone treating her unkindly?*

We can almost visualize Mordecai pacing from one side of the gate to the other, glancing often through the bars to see if he can even catch a glimpse of Esther.

Sitting at the king's gate indicated that Mordecai held a place of respect and authority. He was not just passing by; he had a seat. Is it surprising that God would elevate Mordecai despite his hiding his Jewish heritage?

This scenario is reminiscent of Nicodemus in John 19. He held the respected position of Pharisee, yet he kept secret his interest in Jesus' teachings. Later, when Jesus was crucified and the disciples needed to bury Jesus, what did Nicodemus do in John 19:38–42?

Nicodemus made the decision to step out of the shadows of secret discipleship to declare through his actions that he believed Jesus was the Savior of the world, that Jesus was *his* Savior.

I know what that feels like. At the age of 23, God called me to faith. I was baptized on Palm Sunday 1991 in front of the entire congregation. I could no longer hide what I believed, and I stepped out of the shadows into His glorious light.

But that step did not guarantee an easy path. As I told friends that I had become a Christian, one by one they "forgot" to invite me to certain parties or gatherings. I also declined going to places that would compromise me physically or spiritually. All but two friends faded into the shadows. Over the years, God has replaced those friendship holes with incredible women (and men) of God who hold His agenda in front of their paths. It was a painful yet wonderful transition.

Are there any secret shadows from which you need to step out of? If so, what?

If so, when?

For what purpose has God placed you where you are? Do you wait at the king's gate longing for something else? Or are you seeking His guidance to be used where you are? I have spent many an hour at the gate focused on what my life is missing rather than how God is blessing. We all experience those seasons. The key is ensuring that it's only a season, not a lifetime.

As Mordecai kept vigil at the gate, what happened in Esther 2:21–22?

Oh, the drama! Intrigue and murder have been a part of court life from the time monarchs first existed through today. God placed Mordecai at just the right place and just the right time to prevent the king's assassination.

What did Mordecai do with the information?

Mordecai's actions once again reveal his wisdom. If he had passed along the information through normal court channels, it could have been intercepted by an assassination co-conspirator. A mark of wisdom is knowing to whom and when to reveal information.

Choosing to use Esther as his messenger served two purposes. What do you think they were?

First, Mordecai had been keeping vigil at the gate, so this provided the perfect opportunity to check on Esther and see how she was doing. Also, Esther would ensure that the information was conveyed correctly and properly credited to Mordecai. Second, as a non-native Persian, Mordecai likely wanted to demonstrate his loyalty to and support of Ahasuerus.

When the incident was investigated, what happened in Esther 2:23?

Where was the incident recorded?

So why were such actions recorded in the royal records? It was politically smart. Kings realized that rewarding loyalty was just as important as punishing disloyalty. They realized that most people would extend loyalty for the lure of a reward, which would increase sacrificial acts on behalf of the king. To date, such chronicles from Achaemenid Persia have not yet been discovered.

The two traitorous eunuchs were hanged on the gallows for their treasonous plotting. When most people today hear "gallows," they associate it with an apparatus on which to hang a convicted criminal by the neck like in an old Western. However, the Hebrew word for "gallows" in Esther 2:23 simply means a wooden beam or stake. Historians record that Persians would impale, rather than hang, convicted criminals on these gallows. It served as a public deterrent against similar crimes.

Mordecai saved the life of Ahasuerus who, like the baker in Genesis 40, promptly forgot the man who saved him. Ironically, several years later Ahasuerus would be assassinated by a court official anyway. But by God's providence, that day was delayed because God had plans for Ahasuerus as long as Esther lived in his palace.

Although Mordecai was instrumental in saving the king's life, he did not receive initial acknowledgment or reward. And Mordecai never seeks it either. As God's beloved children, how does Galatians 6:9 encourage believers to live, whether or not we receive worldly gains?

Perhaps you have been waiting to be acknowledged or receive a reward. You wonder when "in due season" will arrive. Hang on, sister! God sees you. In God's perfect timing and God's perfect will, He rewards all who are faithful to Him.

Esther chapter 2 has led us on quite a roller-coaster ride! Through beauty pageants, beauty treatments, harem life, spending one night with the king, and Esther receiving the queen's crown, the story contained more twists than a bread tie. However, one thing remained constant: God's faithful, guiding hand.

As we close the book on this lesson, spend time in prayer. Ask God to reveal to you right now where His hand is guiding you in this season of life. Spend time writing in the margin what He reveals to you.

Keep seeking His face, sister! I'll meet you in Lesson 3.

LESSON 3

When the Enemy Prowls

Esther 3

Every drama needs a villain, and the Book of Esther does not disappoint. Power-hungry with an egotistical chip on his shoulder the size of Mount Everest, Haman enters stage left. When Mordecai bruises Haman's ego by refusing to bow down to him, political storm clouds appear on Susa's horizon. Haman manipulates the king's weak will and passes a vengeful decree to annihilate the entire Jewish population in Persia. As Haman and the king drink to their cleverness, chaos reigns in the streets.

- DAY 1   Haman, the Enemy of the Jews *(Esther 3:1)*
- DAY 2   Destructive Hatred *(Esther 3:2–6)*
- DAY 3   Genocide Decreed *(Esther 3:7–9)*
- DAY 4   Unthinkable Evil *(Esther 3:10–12)*
- DAY 5   Chaos in the Streets *(Esther 3:13–15)*

KEY QUESTIONS

- Would you have urged Mordecai to kneel down to honor Haman rather than risk his life and everyone else's?
- Would you faithfully seek God's direction or follow your own best guess?
- Can God use our wrong decisions for our benefit and His glory?
- When caught in circumstances beyond your control, do you just

go with the flow or take a stand?

- How would you react if you knew your whole race was facing slaughter by the government because of your faith? Would you gather weapons, pray, or do both?

- What three ways does Satan seek to devour believers?

Day 1

Haman, the Enemy of the Jews

After these things King Ahasuerus promoted Haman the Agagite, the son of Hammedatha, and advanced him and set his throne above all the officials who were with him.

(Esther 3:1)

After much preparation and some pomp and circumstance, Esther finally sits next to her royal husband as Persia's new queen. Her cousin Mordecai has foiled an assassination plot against the king, so life seems to be settling down. But drama enters the story once again in the form of the story's villain, Haman, the king's prime minister. As political storm clouds swirl during this lesson, Esther steps into the background and Mordecai moves to center stage, toe-to-toe with Haman.

Read Esther 3:1.

In the original Hebrew narrative, the first trait ascribed to a person when he or she initially appears in the text provides a window into that person's role in the story.

What is Haman's lineage?

We cannot miss how Haman's family background plays a vital role in the narrative. We learned in Lesson 2, Day 2, that Mordecai is a Jew of the tribe of Benjamin (Esther 2:5), descended from Saul through the tribe of Benjamin. Haman is identified here as an Agagite. Let's buckle our chariot seat belts and take a ride through history!

Read 1 Samuel 15:1–22.

What was the name of the Amalekite king in verse 8?

What did the Lord command Saul to do, yet he failed to carry out?

The Amalekite king was named Agag, hence his people were known as Agagites. Haman was an Agagite, therefore a descendant of the Amalekites. God had commanded Saul to strike down every Amalekite plus all of their livestock so that the Amalekites would be wiped from the face of the earth. Yet Saul thought he knew better than God, so he spared the life of their king, Agag.

That is important! So why such a severe judgment? What was the reason behind God's command?

Read Exodus 17:8–16.

What did the Amalekites do to the Israelites?

What did God promise to do to the Amalekites in verse 14?

What was the Israelites' stance regarding the Amalekites?

God's exhausted people were marching their exodus out of Egypt when the Amalekites attacked them in the rear ranks. Consequently, God declared holy war against the Amalekites, promising one day to utterly destroy them for their cowardly attack.

Let's pause for a moment. Has anyone ever been particularly unkind or attacked you when you were already exhausted? If so, what was the circumstance? How did you feel about that person?

After my dad passed away in 2003 following a two-and-a-half-year battle with cancer, I felt completely exhausted physically, emotionally, and spiritually. As I took various days off from work during Dad's illness, a mean girl co-worker decided to start a rumor that I was actually looking for another job. When I found out, I literally could not see straight through my anger. I felt attacked while I was down, and I could feel the bile of rage boil in my soul. It took a lot of prayer and a long time for God to uproot that anger that I had allowed to take root.

It's bad enough for someone to attack you, but attacking you when you're already exhausted adds salt to the wound.

Now read Deuteronomy 25:17–19.

What did the Lord promise to do with the Amalekites?

Following up on His war declaration, God commanded King Saul to destroy all of the Amalekites. However, Saul only halfheartedly followed God's command and allowed some to live. The result? God removed Saul's crown for his disobedience, and Amalekite descendants such as Haman were later born to once again threaten God's chosen people.

There can be long-lasting, even generational, ramifications when we do not follow God's commands. We have only to look at Adam and Eve as proof.

Since Mordecai is a Benjaminite and descended from one of the twelve tribes of Israel, he was an Israelite. The Amalekites (descendants of King Agag) and Israelites (Jews from the Southern Kingdom of Judah) had a long-standing animosity that spanned centuries. This lineage lends crucial insight into understanding the hostility that Haman and Mordecai held against each other.

Since not a single Amalekite (other than King Agag) survived to be an ancestor of Haman, Haman was likely not a direct descendant of Agag, but an Amalekite like Agag who raised himself up against Israel. So 1 Samuel 15 is not referenced to show Haman's descent from Agag, but rather the parallels between the Israelite king Saul overcoming the Amalekite king Agag, and Saul's kinsman Mordecai overcoming Agag's kinsman Haman.

The author of Esther wanted to ensure that we never forgot Haman's lineage, because it's mentioned five times throughout the book. The ancestral baggage between Haman and Mordecai dated back almost a thousand years from when the Jews exited Egypt in 1445 BC. The fatal blow to the Amalekites was carried out by Samuel.

When Saul failed to destroy the Amalekites, what happened in 1 Samuel 15:32–33?

God's keeps His word, period. He promised to avenge the Amalekites' cowardly attack on the exhausted Israelites as they left Egypt. God's curse against the Amalekites resulted in their total elimination as a people (Exodus 17:14).

The enmity between the Amalekites and the Jews reflects the enmity between Haman and Mordecai.

Haman was an Agagite, an Amalekite descendant. Because of his lineage, Haman carried deep hostility toward the Israelites. Consequently, he carried deep hostility—even hatred—for Mordecai the Jew, a Benjaminite. Do you sense trouble brewing? Me too.

According to Esther 3:1, to what position did King Ahasuerus appoint Haman?

Ahasuerus, for reasons unspecified, elevated Haman to second-in-command as prime minister over the entire Persian Empire. The one holding a generational grudge against God's people now holds the second highest office in the land.

This does not bode well for anyone who finds himself on the wrong side of Haman's family tree. And Haman is not in power for long before the claws come out.

As the storm clouds thicken, thank you for persevering through a rather technical lesson. Well done! This background provides a solid historical understanding of the "why" behind the "what" in this epic battle of good versus evil. Knowing this background will help you tremendously in the upcoming lessons.

I love studying the Word with you, sister. Keep going strong!

DAY 2
Destructive Hatred

And all the king's servants who were at the king's gate
bowed down and paid homage to Haman, for the king
had so commanded concerning him. But Mordecai did
not bow down or pay homage. Then the king's servants
who were at the king's gate said to Mordecai, "Why do you
transgress the king's command?" And when they spoke to
him day after day and he would not listen to them, they
told Haman, in order to see whether Mordecai's words
would stand, for he had told them that he was a Jew. And
when Haman saw that Mordecai did not bow down or pay
homage to him, Haman was filled with fury. . . . Haman
sought to destroy all the Jews, the people of Mordecai,
throughout the whole kingdom of Ahasuerus.

(Esther 3:2–6)

The one and only time I saw George W. Bush in person was when he
ran for governor of Texas. Some friends and I had worked on his campaign,
so we (along with thousands of other Texas supporters) were invited to a
rally in Austin as the election approached. He delivered a fantastic speech,
encouraged the troops (and us), and resolved to serve Texas to the best of
his God-given abilities.

When the rally was over, hundreds of people lined his path to offer encouragement and support. People shook his hands, patted him on the back,
hugged him, and kissed his cheek. It was how they showed respect for the
man and the office. He won the election, represented Texas well, and then
went on to become the forty-third president of the United States.

Greetings convey much. Greek historian Herodotus documented the
practice of how Persians typically greeted one another. Those who carried
equal rank greeted each other with a kiss on the mouth. A person holding
a less powerful position would greet a more powerful person with a kiss on
the cheek. However, if their social and/or political status differed greatly,
the lower-ranked person would prostrate himself before the other.

Rank carries respect. For instance, Americans have gone to the polls for over 230 years to elect our US presidents, senators, and congressmen. Though we may not hold the same political affiliation as the candidates chosen, we respect the office to which they have been elected. However, political and moral divisions may stop us short from respecting the individual holding those offices. Welcome to Mordecai's dilemma.

Read Esther 3:2–6.

Where does this scene take place, and who is present?

The story unfolds at the king's gate with *all* the king's servants present. We studied the significance of the city gate in a previous lesson. Much of city life centered around the gate. Even though Ahasuerus had promoted Haman to vizier (prime minister), the king had to command people to bow to Haman. Even though paying homage to leaders and royalty was a common cultural practice, the king had to *instruct* people to respect Haman.

What do you believe that reveals about Haman?

If Haman was an admirable leader, others would have willingly paid proper respect. Walter Savage Landor, a British essayist, once penned: "When little men cast long shadows, it is a sign that the sun is setting."[12]

What is the last sentence in Esther 3:2?

Mordecai acted in a similar way as many of us would today—he made his protest known. We may opt to picket or organize a protest march, but Mordecai opted for the not-so-subtle approach of standing when Haman walked by rather than bowing low as ordered. He did not protest with violence, such as bombing the gate or lobbing rotten fruit. He simply refused to bow. When everyone else bows, it's easy to see who doesn't. Though more passive, Mordecai's resistance was very effective. He never had to utter a word.

The text does not indicate that Mordecai contested bowing to Haman on the basis of worship. In fact, Mordecai had no trouble bowing before Ahasuerus. He had an issue with the person, not the office. A Jewish Targum (interpretive renderings of the books of the Hebrew Scriptures) says that no self-respecting Benjaminite would bow or revere any Amalekite descendant.

We studied this extensively in Lesson 2, Day 2, and it was so important that I asked you to highlight it. Look back there for a moment. Why would a Benjaminite have an issue bowing to an Amalekite?

They were avowed enemies, because God had promised one day to wipe out the Amalekites from the whole earth because of their cowardly attack of the exhausted Israelites as they left Egypt.

We have all lived under the "rule" of an elected official who may not share our values or moral standards, whether a congressman, senator, or president. Mordecai was not the only one in Scripture who defied a king's order.

Read Exodus 1:15–16.

The king of Egypt's rule was law, and to disobey often meant death. However, what did the Hebrew midwives do in Exodus 1:17–19?

The midwives directly defied the king's decree by honoring life and protecting the babies. They were incredibly brave to risk their own lives, because you can't very well hide a screaming baby. They defended life and stood up to the king.

How did God respond to the midwives in Exodus 1:20–21?

God is faithful to those who are faithful to Him. His Word and Gospel message will prevail. When the disciples defied the officials' orders in Jerusalem to cease witnessing about Jesus, how did they respond in Acts 5:29–32?

Faced with such a situation, would you be as brave? It may be easy to say, but much harder to do. Remember the "old" Peter in the Gospels? He promised Jesus that he would never abandon Him, no matter what happened. Yet, when the going got tough and Jesus was arrested, Peter abandoned Jesus in a heartbeat. I don't know about you, but sometimes I find a lot of Peter in me.

As Mordecai refuses to bow, how do those around him react in Esther 3:3–4?

The word *tattletale* comes to mind. The text does not say that the people at the gate were Jew, Gentile, friend, or foe, but they did not like Mordecai's chosen form of rebellion. Why do you believe they would respond in such a way?

Would you have urged Mordecai to kneel down and honor Haman rather than risk wrath by association? Why or why not?

Ahasuerus was the most powerful man in the known world. For anyone who did not follow the king's commands, there were often severe consequences. He had issued a command that people bow down to Haman. So when the king's servants' daily nagging failed to coerce Mordecai into bowing, they reported Mordecai's behavior directly to Haman. Up to that point, Haman had not even noticed Mordecai's protest.

What is Haman's response in Esther 3:5–6?

Haman is the poster boy for how a big person can be so little. If one man's refusal to bow fills you with unreasonable fury, there's a bigger problem than not receiving respect. And the servants added even more fuel to the fire. After Haman had noticed Mordecai's behavior, the king's servants let Haman know that Mordecai was a Jew. I mean, seriously, with co-workers like that, who needs enemies?

We cannot miss the importance of Haman's furious reaction, because this moment reveals the principal plot of the entire Book of Esther.

What did Haman seek to do in Esther 3:6?

Like a malignant tumor, Haman's fury over Mordecai's lack of respect soon manifested into a blind hatred for the whole Jewish population.

Anger is a power source for those who have no real power. There is nothing more dangerous than a powerful, vengeful coward. They tend to victimize those who are weak and lack a powerful protector.

Scholar A. H. Sayce wrote: "Not content with avenging the slight on Mordecai, Haman determined to doom the whole Jewish race to death."[13] At that moment, Haman began devising a calculated attempt to destroy all Persian Jews.

What do you find most disturbing in that fact?

It is horrifying that essentially one man, Haman, decided to attempt genocide of the entire population of Persian Jews during the fifth century BC.

It's even more horrifying to know that essentially one man, Hitler, attempted genocide of the entire population of European Jews within the last century.

Remember that God seems hidden in the Book of Esther, but He's not hiding. Haman would eventually come to realize just how badly he miscalculated the Jews' heavenly Protector. This is not the end of the story; it's only the beginning. God always watches over His children to bring about salvation at just the right time.

For the Jews.

For the Gentiles.

For all who turn their face to Him through faith.

DAY 3
Genocide Decreed

In the first month, which is the month of Nisan, in the twelfth year of King Ahasuerus, they cast Pur (that is, they cast lots) before Haman day after day; and they cast it month after month till the twelfth month, which is the month of Adar. Then Haman said to King Ahasuerus, "There is a certain people scattered abroad and dispersed among the peoples in all the provinces of your kingdom. Their laws are different from those of every other people, and they do not keep the king's laws, so that it is not to the king's profit to tolerate them. If it please the king, let it be decreed that they be destroyed, and I will pay 10,000 talents of silver into the hands of those who have charge of the king's business, that they may put it into the king's treasuries."

(Esther 3:7–9)

Historical timelines are important in stories and life. At this point in the narrative, Ahasuerus has reigned as Persia's king for twelve years, and Esther had been his queen for the last five.

After his humiliating military defeats in Greece, Ahasuerus was likely highly motivated to preserve kingdom cohesion. Maintaining such unity hinged on controlling citizens through carefully enforced laws. And one of those laws, or commands, involved the king's newly appointed prime minister, Haman the Agagite.

He had just been appointed prime minister and second-in-command under Ahasuerus. He had also just noticed that Mordecai the Jew refused to pay him the honor commanded by the king. We left off in Esther 3:6 with Haman's ominous intentions from the last lesson still ringing in our ears: *Haman sought to destroy all the Jews.* Now it was time for Haman to make those intentions a reality.

Read Esther 3:7–9.

Haman employs his arsenal of slithery skills to persuade Ahasuerus to decree anti-Semitic annihilation. Not once did Haman mention that these "certain people" happened to be the entire race of Judeans living in Persia.

Haman explicitly avoided placing any religious affiliation to them because Persian kings were known for their tolerance and diversity. When you're trying to get your way, wording matters. It would be politically damaging for Ahasuerus to stand against an entire people group, much less to order their liquidation. Even in today's volatile politics, it would be the death of an American politician's career to come out against an entire people group based on ethnicity or religion.

When I was a girl, my parents bought my three sisters and me one of those Magic 8-Balls that were popular in the 1970s. It was a plastic ball about twice the size of a grapefruit that was designed to look like an eight-ball. It was filled with a blue liquid and a white floating multisided orb on which were written general answers.

The game was to ask the Magic 8-Ball a question, shake it, and wait for the answer to float to the surface in the little glass window. My sisters and I would ask it all sorts of questions: *Will I have to go to school tomorrow? Will I get what I want for Christmas?* Simple, innocent kid questions. The Magic 8-Ball offered general answers: *Outlook good. My sources say no.* And the most frustrating one: *Better not tell you now.*

This silly game provided much amusement when we asked questions like this: *Will Mom make (insert sister's name) do the dishes tonight instead of me?* So why are we talking about Magic 8-Balls? Because a similar practice has occurred for millennia.

According to Esther 3:7, what was the first thing that Haman did to put his plan in motion?

Casting lots was a common practice, much like rolling the dice today. *Pur* is the Babylonian word for "lots." Archaeologists have unearthed one-inch-square cubes dating to Ahasuerus's reign, which usually contained prayer inscriptions for good luck rather than plain dots. Similar cubes have been discovered that date back to the third millennium.

Tradition holds that lots were cast in the first month of each year to reveal the most opportune time for significant events during the coming year. Haman followed that tradition when he cast lots in the first month. Some speculate that pur was cast onto a board that contained each month's name. The answer usually needed to appear in three consecutive throws to be authoritative (if such a word can be construed with ancient dice). The date finally chosen for Haman's genocidal plan was eleven months in the future.

Eleven months! He would have to endure Mordecai's insolent behavior for almost a year. That's a long time for a furious person to wait for revenge. Fury and time are a dangerous cocktail.

The Old Testament reveals that people in the ancient Near East routinely consulted stars, omens, and other factors to determine a course of action. For example, when Nebuchadnezzar wanted confirmation of which road to take in battle, what did he do according to Ezekiel 21:21?

What did the sailors discover in Jonah 1:7 after they cast lots?

Casting lots was still practiced into the New Testament. For what purpose did the guards cast lots in Luke 23:33–34?

For what purpose did the disciples cast lots in Acts 1:24–26?

Haman's casting pur was not to ask a simple, innocent kid question. It was to determine which day would be favorable for his genocidal plot against Persian Jews to be set in motion. Little did Haman know that God was in control of those ancient dice.

Write Proverbs 16:33.

We can clearly see God's hand rolling Haman's dice because He set the date almost a year away to allow His people adequate time to prepare. It also provided the time God desired to orchestrate some key events in the lives of our main characters.

Read Esther 3:8.

Haman's indictment to the king against the Jews is a combination of truth, lies, and exaggeration. Mark which was truth (T), lies (L), and exaggeration (E) in each statement:

_____ **Certain people scattered abroad and dispersed.**

_____ **Their laws** (*customs*) **are different from those of every other people**

_____ **They do not keep the king's laws.**

Notice the deterioration from truth to outright lie. The Jews are indeed dispersed, but only some of their customs were different. However, they obeyed the laws of the land, because if the Persian Jews were consistent troublemakers, Ahasuerus would have been aware of it and historians would have recorded it. However, the king did not bother to take the time to weigh the truth of Haman's accusations.

In Esther 3:9, what does Haman ask the king to do to the Jews?

How mad does someone need to be in order to say a phrase such as *"let it be decreed that they be destroyed"* and then continue on to talk about the money to finance it? Haman's lack of regard for life is stunning. Also he was obviously not above a bribe to achieve his self-centered agenda. If the diviners and fortune-tellers had not worked to persuade King Ahasuerus to commit genocide, Haman was willing to shell out cold, hard cash. A *lot* of cash.

What monetary sum did Haman offer the king?

Since the majority of us are a little rusty on the worth of 10,000 talents of silver, let's indulge in some helpful calculations. A talent equals 75 pounds, so 10,000 talents equals 750,000 pounds. There are 14.58 troy ounces of silver per pound. When we multiply 14.58 times 750,000 we arrive at 10,935,000 troy ounces of silver. Priced at a rough current market value of $21.31 per ounce, Haman's bribe would be the equivalent of over $233 million today.

That was the weight of Haman's hate.

The historian Herodotus reported that the Persian Empire's total annual income was around fifteen thousand talents of silver. Haman's ten-thousand talent bribe constituted a whopping two-thirds of the empire's total annual income. Offering this much money to the king reveals two important facts about Haman: (1) he possessed enormous wealth, and (2) he expected to recoup his losses by pillaging the murdered Jews. It is easy to conclude that Haman intended to benefit from plundering the Jews in order to refill his coffers.

As we reach the end of this sobering lesson, you and I live in a world where such hate runs unchecked in parts of the world. As God's children, we know that Satan is the ruler of this world (John 12:31; 2 Corinthians 4:4). However, God has not left us defenseless. He has given us His armor (Ephesians 6:10–18) and His might through the power of the Holy Spirit.

God alone holds ultimate control over those who receive authority, whether Haman, Nebuchadnezzar, Nero, Pontius Pilate, Hitler, or Osama bin Laden. And though such authority can be horribly abused, we live under the Authority who always works for our good.

You don't have to cast lots or shake a Magic 8-Ball to reveal whether or not God knows and cares about you. Regardless of hard circumstances, God promises to bring good out of every single one. And you can take that to the spiritual bank, sisters.

DAY 4
Unthinkable Evil

So the king took his signet ring from his hand and gave it to Haman the Agagite, the son of Hammedatha, the enemy of the Jews. And the king said to Haman, "The money is given to you, the people also, to do with them as it seems good to you." Then the king's scribes were summoned on the thirteenth day of the first month, and an edict, according to all that Haman commanded, was written to the king's satraps and to the governors over all the provinces and to the officials of all the peoples, to every province in its own script and every people in its own language. It was written in the name of King Ahasuerus and sealed with the king's signet ring.

(Esther 3:10–12)

The term *diaspora* comes from an ancient Greek word meaning "to scatter about." In the Bible, the Jewish Diaspora refers to the dispersion of God's chosen people to countries outside of their ancestral land of Israel following the Babylonian captivity.

One of the most interesting facts about the Book of Esther is that it reveals a vastly different lifestyle between the Judeans who returned to Jerusalem to rebuild after Cyrus released them from exile and the Diaspora-era Israelites who chose to remain in the luxurious Persian Empire.

Mordecai became politically successful as he remained in Persia and worked with the Gentiles. He also worked with exiled Jews to form a faithful community within Persia. Such faithful work put Mordecai in an excellent position to be used by God to save His people from genocide.

Haman has just asked the king to decree the annihilation of all Persian Jews and offered him an exorbitant amount to persuade the king. Let's pick up our story.

Read Esther 3:10–12.

How is Haman identified?

For the first time, we see in black and white that Haman was "the enemy of the Jews." This is the point in the story when the ominous sound of the orchestra's tympani begins to swell. The author did not want the reader to forget the long history of animosity between the Amalekites and Israelites.

Without even asking Haman for evidence or performing his own due diligence, what did Ahasuerus hand over to Haman without hesitation in Esther 3:10?

As the king passed his signet ring to Haman, the author emphasizes once again the triple threat that Haman poses to the Persian Jews. Fill in the blanks:

> "So the king took his signet ring from his hand and gave it to Ha-
> man the _____, the son of _____,
> the _____ of the Jews."

As we learned last lesson, the Agagites were mortal enemies of the Benjaminites. That triple threat originated from Haman's lineage and family line. Haman also posed a political triple threat: (1) power, (2) position, and (3) the ear of the king. While Haman had little to do with the first set of triple threats, this second set proves his intent as the architect of genocide.

In a moment that reveals an uninterested, weak king, Ahasuerus blindly turned over his signet ring to Haman. By that seemingly insignificant action, the king consented to the indiscriminate, mass slaughter of every Persian Jew—man, woman, and child.

It is tantamount today to the California man who, several years ago, left his campfire coals burning and continued on his hike. The resulting raging forest fire sparked by his campfire eventually cost dozens of lives and destroyed thousands of acres. The fire was unintentional. No such innocent accident can be attributed to Haman's actions.

Historians confirm that a king's signet ring was used to mark or secure documents of importance. They were often made from chalcedony (a microcrystalline type of quartz similar to onyx, agate, and jasper) and usually boasted images of the king performing heroic acts.

The king would press his signet ring into softened wax on the outside of a scroll, and that wax would harden into an official, unbroken seal. The ring's seal represented the king's power, authority, and personal guarantee of the scroll's contents, making it highly valued. Archaeologists have uncovered only a few royal signet rings from ancient times.

In **Esther 3:12,** what date is mentioned?

The author uses literary artistry to reveal a date that only the Israelites would recognize. On the ancient calendar, the first month was Nisan. The king's scribes were summoned to write the edict on the thirteenth day of the month of Nisan. The fourteenth day of Nisan was the first day of Passover, when the Israelites celebrated their liberation from Egyptian slavery.

The irony is unambiguous. At the precise time when the Jews would be celebrating deliverance from their Egyptian enemy of the past, they received a decree announcing plans for their destruction from a Persian enemy of the present.

Have you ever been prepared to celebrate an anticipated event only to receive devastating news instead? What happened?

Those moments are hard to articulate because so many emotions hit at once. Several years ago, one of our church's mission teams had just returned from a mission trip to Honduras. I was looking forward to hearing the incredible ways they saw God move. Instead, I received a call telling me that one of the mission team members had been killed in a car accident the night before. He was the only child of a well-liked couple on our church staff. Moments like those freeze time and etch every feeling on our heart.

Once Haman's date of genocide had been set and approved by Ahasuerus, the king's scribes wrote and disbursed the edict for immediate distribution throughout the land. Using their impressive communication "Pony Express" system that we studied in Lesson 1, Day 5 (when the king dispersed a message commanding all women to respect their husbands), to whom was the king's decree sent according to Esther 3:12?

Did you notice that the decree was not disseminated to the general population? It was *specifically* sent to the king's satraps, governors, and officials over the provinces, and officials over the people. That represents an important distinction. Esther 3:9 provides a vital clue.

In Esther 3:9, who would receive Haman's bribe money?

Historians record that each Persian province supplied soldiers for the Persian Empire's military might who conducted the king's business on his behalf. Consequently, the king's decree did not offer "general" slaughter of the Jews by civilians; rather, the mission was entrusted to those who specifically possessed military skills.

As we close another hard day's lesson, remember that even in the face of terrible news—in your life or the Persian Jews—the situation is never hopeless because God is never absent.

You may not see His hand at work and may wonder why bad things happen to faithful followers, but God is still working.

Close in prayer by asking God to give you the eyes of faith to see His hand in your life right now.

DAY 5
Chaos in the Streets

Letters were sent by couriers to all the king's provinces with instruction to destroy, to kill, and to annihilate all Jews, young and old, women and children, in one day, the thirteenth day of the twelfth month, which is the month of Adar, and to plunder their goods. A copy of the document was to be issued as a decree in every province by proclamation to all the peoples to be ready for that day. The couriers went out hurriedly by order of the king, and the decree was issued in Susa the citadel. And the king and Haman sat down to drink, but the city of Susa was thrown into confusion.

(Esther 3:13–15)

Grandma Headlee immigrated to the United States from Germany in 1942 as Hitler's power rose. After knowing my grandpa for years, they wed after my real grandma died of cancer before I was born. Even though Grandma Headlee was my step-grandma, she was the only grandma I knew on my mom's side of the family.

She grew up in a small Lutheran town in Germany. After witnessing Hitler's genocide of the Jews for almost a decade, her family set sail for the United States to start a new life in safer surroundings. Though Grandma Headlee never talked about it, I learned when I became an adult that she lost family and friends in Hitler's campaigns of human extinction. She witnessed firsthand the effects of a horror that we cannot fully fathom even now, more than eight decades later.

Hitler set up his first concentration camp in March 1933 in the town of Dachau, just outside the city of Munich. Most of the camps ran continuously until military troops in World War II began liberating prisoners in 1945. *Twelve years and over six million deaths.* When terrible events like that happen without an end in sight, does it sometimes seem that God has stepped out to grab some coffee?

Read Esther 3:13–15.

Haman had a lot in common with Hitler. The author's detailed description of Haman's plot to kill the Jews is so strong you can almost smell death approaching. Esther's palace life was now fragrant with the lethal toxins of Hitler's gas chambers.

Imagine living in Persia as a Jew and hearing the news that your death has been decreed. It would have been tantamount to an ISIS terrorist leader being appointed president of the United States and invoking Sharia law.

In Esther 3:13, whom were the Persian military authorized to kill?

It turns my stomach to see children on that list. Similar to Hitler, Haman's chief criteria that selected entire family units for slaughter was the fact that they were Jews.

Clearly, Satan is involved. Satan knew of God's promised redemption and moved in lethal forces to wipe out the covenantal, redemptive line of descent. In effect, Satan sounded the war cry. What does Ephesians 6:12 say about this unseen yet very real war?

Historically, Scripture clearly reveals that all who have persecuted Jews have inevitably experienced destruction.

What does 2 Kings 19:30–31 tell us about God's protection of His children?

Even as God protected His chosen people, He protects all who believe by faith that Jesus died and rose again to secure a place for us in heaven. No matter who or what aligns against us on earth, nothing happens apart from God's watchful gaze.

And God sees everything, including what's about to happen in our story. Write out the last phrase in Esther 3:13.

Part of the decree Haman constructed was to allow those who attacked the Jews to also plunder their goods. Why is that important? As my tour guide/political expert friend, Ori, astutely noted:

> Looting is an important motive when seeking to urge attacks against a distinct group of people. In fact, it is a means to motivate people to do particularly criminal acts.[14]

Those military men who may have balked at attacking women and children may have given it a second thought if they were awarded the opportunity to line their pockets and furnish their homes with plunder.

The Hebrew word for "plunder" *(bazaz)* means to snatch away or take a prey. The primary power in the word indicates "to pull in pieces." When someone's possessions are plundered, their possessions are pulled in pieces (much like when the soldiers divided Jesus' garments among them and cast lots for His robe). When someone's physical person is plundered, their lives are pulled in pieces. Both are sobering scenarios on many levels.

That verb for plunder appears over forty times in the Old Testament. Often, it is used of the plunder that God allowed the Israelites to capture. However, here in Esther 3:13 and another significant occurrence in Scripture, plunder references when God's people will be the ones affected.

Write out Jeremiah 20:5.

God used the word *plunder* to describe His judgment against the Israelites' unfaithfulness as they were carried into Babylonian captivity for seventy years. God again pronounces similar doom against His people ten chapters later: *"Because your guilt is great, because your sins are flagrant, I have done these things to you"* (Jeremiah 30:16).

Even when the offenders are His children, God corrects those He loves.

Write out Proverbs 3:12.

Now write out Hebrews 12:6.

God disciplines those He loves *precisely because* He loves them. When you and I walk in sinful ways, God will not stand idly by, because such pathways lead away from Him. He created us to enjoy intimate fellowship with Him, so anything that stands in the way has to be removed.

Haman's genocidal decree has been signed, sealed, and sent out. Once the copies of the decree are on their way, what do the king and Haman do according to Esther 3:15?

While citizens across Persia staggered in bewilderment, Ahasuerus and Haman sat down to drink in bliss. How creepy is that? It is tantamount to a champagne toast over a coffin at a funeral while mourners weep.

Some Persians may have harbored anti-Semitic feelings, but there is a clear air of bewilderment and confusion throughout the empire, not just among the Jews. The Persian Empire was comprised of many ethnicities, so perhaps citizens believed that if the king could make such a decree against one people group, he could do the same against theirs.

There is no room allowed in God's world to hate, especially racial ethnicities. Christians need to be the first to step up when we witness such anti-Semitic or racist behavior because we lead with God's love.

As we reach the end of studying Esther 3, we see how hatred creates an opportunity to turn someone's normal day into their last. What you and I need to wrestle with as Christians is that the sins of hatred, malice, and greed are not unique to Haman. They exist in our world today and even inside of us.

Hatred is taught. So is love.

Hatred is demonstrated. So is love.

Hatred will prevail as long as love stands silent.

For Haman, his power rested in the complete destruction of the Jews.

But Haman had not yet encountered the power of Esther's God.

LESSON 4

Chosen for Such a Time as This

Esther 4

Esther's story contains all the elements of a fairy tale and often gets treated as one—part Cinderella, part Beauty and the Beast—especially considering all the feasting and parties. A beautiful maiden comes out of obscurity to win the king's heart and become his bride. The king falls under the spell of the evil villain Haman, but he is eventually freed by the courageous resourcefulness of his enchanting queen. Perhaps it is a longing for the "happily ever after" in our own stories that leaves us clinging to fairy-tale interpretations of the Bible. But Esther's story was not a fairy tale; in reality, it was much closer to a nightmare.

- **DAY 1**   The King's Decree: Mordecai's Response *(Esther 4:1–3)*

- **DAY 2**   The King's Decree: Esther's Response *(Esther 4:4–5)*

- **DAY 3**   When Fear Interferes *(Esther 4:6–11)*

- **DAY 4**   God's Providence *(Esther 4:12–14)*

- **DAY 5**   If I Perish, I Perish *(Esther 4:15–17)*

KEY QUESTIONS

- How does Esther's story show us that God values and works through us, despite adversity, to advance His kingdom today?

- Can you imagine a crisis in which you would go against the law, as Esther did, to actively find a solution?

- Esther was caught between the Gentile world in which she lived and the Jewish world in which she was raised. Can you think of a defining moment in your life based on your self-identification as one of God's people?

DAY 1

The King's Decree: Mordecai's Response

When Mordecai learned all that had been done, Mordecai tore his clothes and put on sackcloth and ashes, and went out into the midst of the city, and he cried out with a loud and bitter cry. He went up to the entrance of the king's gate, for no one was allowed to enter the king's gate clothed in sackcloth. And in every province, wherever the king's command and his decree reached, there was great mourning among the Jews, with fasting and weeping and lamenting, and many of them lay in sackcloth and ashes.

(Esther 4:1–3)

Can you imagine reading your own death warrant months ahead of your scheduled execution? I can't, but one of my pastors can. It was not unusual for Tim in his former career.

For several years, Tim Carter, author of *The Executioner's Redemption,* served as captain of the prison guard for Texas death row inmates. His job was to ensure that court-ordered executions were carried out timely with no disruption. During his tenure in that very difficult position, he and the prison chaplain spent the last few hours with dozens of inmates before escorting them to their death.

Tim was surrounded daily by convicted felons awaiting execution. Every person in that cellblock knew their death date months or even years before it happened. Some reacted by continuing their violent behavior inside the prison as they had lived outside of it. Some reacted by shutting down or becoming overwhelmed emotionally. However, some reacted by reaching out to God for the first time in their lives.

The Jews in Persia had received their death warrant for mass execution by the king's couriers just as they were looking forward to celebrating Passover.

Read Esther 4:1–3.

What was Mordecai's reaction?

We never know how we will react to life-altering news until we receive it. Scripture records several instances where someone in deep grief or repentance visibly expressed sorrow through tearing their garments, adorning sackcloth, and sprinkling ashes on their head. It was also a practice that was historically documented from Mesopotamia and Canaan, as well as throughout the Old Testament (Genesis 37:33–34; Job 2:7–8; Isaiah 3:24; Daniel 9:3).

What were such occasions of grief in the following passages?

2 Samuel 1:11–12

Job 1:13–20

Job 2:11–13

Each story reflects grieving at the death or radically altered lives of loved ones. Those significant losses can throw us into a pit of deepest grief. I tend to be a very private person when I grieve. I usually share those ugly cry moments with God, my family, and a few close friends.

On occasions when you have experienced deep sorrow, how and with whom have you expressed your grief?

Part of life on this earth is experiencing grief. I remember the very moment when I received word one afternoon several years ago that a dear friend who had served as one of my bridesmaids committed suicide. That loss felt like a sword in my gut. That season was hard to walk through, but it was just a season. Those terrible moments do not have to define our life; rather, when we allow God to minister to us, they can be seasons of immense spiritual growth and strengthening.

After Haman's evil plan to annihilate the Jews received the king's irrevocable seal of approval, Mordecai put on sackcloth and ashes and mourned with his fellow Judeans.

However, in addition to tearing his clothes and putting on sackcloth and ashes, where did Mordecai express his sorrow according to Esther 4:2?

Remember the importance of a city gate? Mordecai's grief, in part, was intentional to garner as much attention as possible to the Jews' dire predicament. And he knew the perfect location for such a display. The one place where everything important transpired: the city gate.

What activities routinely took place at the city's gate? (Hint: You can look back at Lesson 2, Day 5.)

Mordecai was wearing ashes and sackcloth in his grief. What did Esther 4:2 say about sackcloth?

Mordecai carried his grief all the way to the king's gate, even while wearing sackcloth. On the surface, such grief-induced meandering may seem random. However, by grieving publicly at the very hub of commercial, social, and judicial dealings, Mordecai's actions proclaimed that he was a Jew who was unafraid to denounce—and even combat—the king's unjustified, deadly decree. *The Lutheran Study Bible* describes activities at a city's gate this way:

> In the ancient Near East, the elders of a community would typically hold court in a city gate (Jb 29:7). In the ancient city of Gezer, archaeologists have found stone benches in the gate chambers where the elders sat. The elders likely wore garments that distinguished their service (Jb 29:14). Parties in dispute would approach them at the gate, explain their case, and count on a wise ruling.[15]

At a city's gate, people conducted business, aired grievances, formed important alliances, received the latest news, socialized, and made one's opinion known. And boy howdy, Mordecai was making his opinion known! He had positioned himself in the most important, public location to draw the most attention to the king's horrid decree.

But he was not the only person grieving.

Write out Esther 4:3.

Can you imagine the outcry of grief? Tens of thousands of Judeans grieved simultaneously upon learning of their impending doom. We know by now that the Book of Esther does not mention God by name. However, how does Esther 4:3 make a veiled reference to God?

The Jews fasted. When people mourned or repented through fasting, prayer usually accompanied it. As they fasted (and as people fast today), the usual practice was (is) to devote the time formerly spent on eating to prayer, seeking God and His guidance.

The Jews were devoted to God, so why was He allowing this to happen? When scenarios do not play out as we choose, our rash or angry response may be to blame God. After all, He's in charge, right? Who else is to blame?

Have you ever blamed God for anything? If so, what and why?

Would Mordecai have been justified to believe that God had turned against him and his people? Why or why not?

Since we believe in an ultimate good, we must believe in an ultimate evil. We take comfort in the fact that God arranges His servants and restrains our enemies. God's enemies can never do more than God permits. Remember Job?

According to Job 1:6–12, why was Job caused to suffer?

When all was said and done, God restored Job's fortunes to "twice as much as he had before" (Job 42:10). God tests the faith of His children, not to destroy us, but to strengthen us (James 1:2–5).

It was illegal to show grief in the presence of the king because he wanted to be isolated from the sorrows of his people. In beautiful contrast, Jesus did not shut off our sorrows; rather, He took them upon Himself. Jesus was not afraid or uncomfortable to comfort us when we mourn and grieve.

Mordecai, Esther, and all Persian Jews were being tested on a life-and-death scale. True courage during trials comes only from the Lord. Lasting change originates solely from Him. And salvation for the Jews and for all of us comes from one person—Jesus Christ.

DAY 2
The King's Decree: Esther's Response

When Esther's young women and her eunuchs came and
told her, the queen was deeply distressed. She sent garments to clothe Mordecai, so that he might take off his
sackcloth, but he would not accept them. Then Esther
called for Hathach, one of the king's eunuchs, who had
been appointed to attend her, and ordered him to go to
Mordecai to learn what this was and why it was.

(Esther 4:4–5)

As the curtain opens on this scene, Esther finally slips back onto the
stage once again. Five long years have passed since the queen's crown had
been placed on Esther's lovely head. She was fully ensconced in court life,
and nothing in our story indicates that any momentous event had happened. Her life was sailing on smooth waters, but the winds of change were
about to swoop in with hurricane-force turbulence.

Read Esther 4:4–5.

Who brought Esther the message about Mordecai?

What news did they tell her? (Hint: Look back at 4:1.)

What was Esther's initial response?

Esther was "deeply distressed." The original Hebrew for "deeply distressed" is translated from "writhed in great anguish" *(chuwl maod shalach)*, a word often used to describe a woman in labor and giving birth. Esther was not merely disturbed at Mordecai's behavior as an annoyance. She was *deeply distressed.*

What situation in your life (apart from childbirth) has caused you distress to such a degree?

What was the result?

The word for *distressed* here is the same word used by King Darius (Ahasuerus's father) when he called out to Daniel from outside the lions' den to find out whether or not Daniel had survived the night.

What happened in Daniel 6:20?

Distressed is the same word that Paul uses in Romans to convey great sorrow and anguish. What was the occasion according to Romans 9:1–5?

Such deep distress and writhing can disturb us to the core of our soul. Esther was not merely annoyed or bothered by the fact that Mordecai was parading in front of the king's gate in sackcloth and ashes.

When Esther received word about Mordecai's behavior at the gate, besides being distressed, what was the first thing she did?

Many women think of fashion first. Some may view Esther as an ungrateful, rescued Israelite who forgot God in the face of luxurious surroundings. However, her reason for sending clothes has a far greater purpose than outward adornment. During her years in the king's palace, Esther had come to understand the king and court etiquette very well. She was concerned about her cousin because she realized there may be trouble if Mordecai's behavior was noticed by the king.

Hathach, one of the king's eunuchs, was serving Esther in her royal capacity, and he is named here as one of the messengers regarding Mordecai's situation. Notice that he did not take the message to the king. We cannot put a price on discretion, especially in this situation.

As Esther had won favor in the harem before being crowned queen, she must have continued winning favor. Significantly, Esther must have placed great trust in Hathach, because up to that point, her Jewish lineage had still not been made public. Right here we see Esther taking her first risk as queen.

Reread Esther 4:5.

What is the first word of the verse?

Then is a time word. It means events have just transpired that inform, as radio broadcaster Paul Harvey used to say, "the rest of the story." First Esther learned of Mordecai's distress, and *then* she did what many of us attempt to do: fix the problem in her own strength. She tried to fix the perceived problem without taking time to understand the real problem. She did not yet fully understand the all-encompassing scope of the reason behind Mordecai's mourning.

Have you ever tried to fix an issue with a knee-jerk reaction without fully knowing the situation or facts? If so, what happened?

God's perfect timing is an integral part of a believer's life. I am guilty of attempting to rush that process more often than I care to admit. When we just want a problem to go away as quickly as possible, stopping to consider all angles sometimes falls far down the list as a casualty of being expeditious.

In Esther 4:5, what did Esther order Hathach to do?

By God's providence, Esther took that extra step to discover *why* Mordecai was upset. Esther could have silently fretted in ignorance. She could have merely assumed possible reasons. She could have shared her baseless assumptions with her maids so that they could needlessly fret together. And she could have done nothing.

Esther did what Ahasuerus never did: open honest lines of communication. Taking that extra step is vital as we navigate life on this planet. The world can be a cold place if all we do is observe someone's suffering at arm's length without communicating and offering meaningful assistance based on the actual needs. We need one another. That's how God wired us.

Many things in this world can alarm us: the economy, politics, pandemics, apathy, terrorism, and so many other issues. Standing in the gap for one another, and trusting God to get us through together, is the only way we will survive.

When you become alarmed by things of this world, what do you normally do?

These verses instruct us to handle those tidal waves of life. Take a moment to write out each one and allow time to reread them a few times.

Isaiah 41:13

Psalm 34:18

Deuteronomy 31:8

When storms hit, we can allow fear to debilitate us into ineffectiveness, or we can hit our knees in prayer. I admit that I'm a fixer. I'm an organizer. Like Esther, I first try to solve issues in my own feeble strength.

The coronavirus pandemic across the globe in 2020 comes to mind. I prayed daily and asked God to intervene and stop it. I also searched news channels and websites to keep up-to-the-minute on unfolding cases. Yes, being informed is smart, but there is a point when too much information can sideline us emotionally, spiritually, and physically. There comes a time when we need to step out and *do* something. Here Esther becomes a *doer*.

When Mordecai refused the clothes that Esther sent to the gate, she sent someone she trusted to find out what was going on. Esther did not walk around the palace asking others what they thought, because second- and thirdhand information is often unreliable. She loved her cousin and wanted to know from him and no one else what was happening.

Haman's actions had caused uproar at the city gate and mourning across Persia.

However, God had placed Esther and Mordecai in place at just the right moment in time to be His instruments of change.

As we wrap up today's lesson take time to ponder this question: How has God put you where you are today to be His instrument for change?

DAY 3
When Fear Interferes

Mordecai also gave him a copy of the written decree issued
in Susa for their destruction, that he might show it to
Esther and explain it to her and command her to go to the
king to beg his favor and plead with him on behalf of her
people. And Hathach went and told Esther what Mordecai
had said. Then Esther spoke to Hathach and commanded
him to go to Mordecai and say, "All the king's servants and
the people of the king's provinces know that if any man or
woman goes to the king inside the inner court without being called, there is but one law—to be put to death, except
the one to whom the king holds out the golden scepter so
that he may live. But as for me, I have not been called to
come in to the king these thirty days."

(Esther 4:8–11)

Esther trying to clothe a grieving Mordecai. Drama in the streets. Drama at the city gate. What a scene we left off in yesterday's lesson!

As the drama ramps up even further today, so does fear. Fear is a thief
of life that causes us to hide behind what is safe rather than stepping out in
faith. And Esther's faith is about to be tested.

Read Esther 4:6–8.

Who is the first person mentioned in verse 6?

God often uses minor players in the story to accomplish major tasks.
Hathach, the king's eunuch assigned to Esther, was simply following orders
to relay notes between Esther and Mordecai. However, his contribution
swung wide the door for a grander goal. At least we know his name. That is
not always the case, however.

For instance, what was the name of the boy who surrendered to Jesus his meager lunch of five loaves and two fish (John 6:1–13)? Who were the men who lifted Paul to safety in a basket over the Damascus wall (Acts 9:23–25)? They are nameless yet important players on God's chessboard.

Mordecai's wise refusal of new clothes opened a perfect window to let Esther know what was happening. He also possessed another interesting fact about the king's decree. In Esther 4:7, what did Mordecai know?

Such intimate knowledge reveals that Mordecai was not merely a junior courtier but a man of influence and trust. Though he was mourning, Mordecai came to Esther with a copy of the king's decree.

The Apocrypha (mentioned at the beginning of this study), sets forth the wording of the decree:

> We understand that this [Jewish] nation, and it alone, stands constantly in opposition to all, perversely following a strange manner of life and laws and is ill disposed to our government, doing all the harm they can so that our kingdom may not attain stability. Therefore, we have decreed that those indicated to you in the letters of Haman, who is in charge of affairs and is our second father, shall all, with their wives and children, be utterly destroyed by the sword of their enemies, without pity or mercy, on the fourteenth day of the twelfth month, Adar, of this present year, so that those who have long been and are now hostile may in one day go down in violence to Hades and leave our government completely secure and untroubled hereafter.
>
> (Addition B, 13:5–7)[16]

Take a moment to reread the decree. What aspects do you find most disturbing?

Slander, inaccuracies, and hate ooze from every accusation. The decree is specifically designed to be destructive and deadly. Nothing is vague or implied; Haman wanted no room for misinterpretation. Malice suffers no typos.

Mordecai did not show a copy of the king's decree just for information. According to the last part of Esther 4:8, what did Mordecai expect Esther to do?

Mordecai's instruction for Esther to approach the king gives insight into his character. Mordecai was not a stand-by-and-watch kind of guy. When he identified a problem he could help solve, he moved toward that solution. We see evidence of his mindset when he took in Esther after her parents died. He could have chosen to let her be placed in an orphanage or with other family members. Instead, Mordecai stepped up and adopted her.

People with a "get-er-done" mindset tend to raise children with the same mindset. Perhaps Mordecai had raised Esther to be a problem solver instead of a bystander. It would certainly explain why he took the decree to Esther and not to another court official to petition the king.

Read Esther 4:9–11.

It is important to note that these are Esther's *first spoken words* since this whole drama began. We are *four chapters* into the story. What does that say about Esther?

Listeners tend to be much smarter because they have taken the time to pay attention to more than people's words. Take a moment to list the highlights of what Esther says:

The fear in Esther's words is almost palpable. She has been the king's wife long enough to be intimately familiar with court etiquette and rules. Approaching the king uninvited was a life-threatening no-no.

According to verse 11, what does the king have to do in order to spare the life of an uninvited court visitor?

Archaeologists have uncovered numerous illustrations of Persian kings holding long scepters as they held court. Esther 4:11 makes clear two important facts: (1) *all* the people throughout Persia knew about the scepter; and (2) this was the law. Esther was not simply letting her imagination feed her fear. Unlike Haman's imagined threat of the Jewish population, Esther was facing a real possibility of death.

In chapter 1, we see Vashti refusing to approach the king when invited. How does this contrast with Esther's situation?

In Ahasuerus's eyes, Esther may have been just as disposable as Vashti. We only have to look at what happened. Vashti caused the king embarrassment and was unceremoniously yanked out of the story. What if Esther approaching the king uninvited caused him embarrassment?

Fear can immobilize us into inaction. When we run all of the "what if" scenarios through our mind, our feet can become glued to the carpet.

Knowing Jesus as Lord and Savior has the power to erase all of our fear. Write out the following passages regarding what God tells us about fear:

Luke 12:32

Matthew 14:27

1 John 4:18–19

Those 1 John verses are particularly relevant to Esther's situation. Perfect love casts out fear, but perhaps she did not know such love from her husband. Our source of fearlessness and perfect love is freely given by God through Jesus Christ. He came to sacrifice His life for us so that our joy in salvation could be made full—not to allow fear to run amuck.

This brings up the question of Esther's access to the king or lack thereof. Even though she was Ahasuerus's queen, she did not routinely share his bed, and they dined separately. Esther also resided in private quarters apart from the king. The most powerful woman in the kingdom still had to request an audience to spend time with her husband.

What does the last sentence of Esther 4:11 say?

Developing an intimate relationship with your spouse is an integral part of a fulfilling, strong marriage. Such intimacy transcends the bedroom to experience life together. However, Esther was allowed in his presence (and in his bedroom) only when summoned.

Would you be able to thrive in a marital arrangement like Esther? Why or why not?

Many commentators have pondered the reasons why Esther chose not to follow the proper channels to obtain an audience with Ahasuerus. She could have simply waited until the king called her in the natural course of time. However, since Haman held the office of prime minister, Esther would have been required to submit her request through his office, thereby endangering the entire mission.

Throughout our story so far, Esther has been silent for the most part. She submitted to being selected as a contestant in the Miss Persia contest. She submitted to Mordecai's instructions not to reveal her lineage. She submitted to the advice of the harem's chief eunuch on how to win the king's heart and crown. She submitted to the custom and spent one night with the king as an unmarried virgin. Esther was quiet. As a woman living in a generation where her voice was not given credibility, perhaps she chose never to use her voice at all.

Do you struggle with choosing not to use your voice? If so, how? Why?

There is a time and a place to be silent, but there is also a time and a place to be heard. Esther's default position to remain quiet and unobtrusive could prove to be a significant stumbling block. She needed to use her brains instead of her beauty and her cunning instead of her charm in order to stand firm in God's strength. Such things require a voice. Perhaps this is the moment when Esther, having long lost her voice, finally relied on God's strength to find it again.

Esther, Mordecai, and the Persian Jews may have been caught off guard by the king's decree, but God had already prepared what they would need to survive and thrive. We see that truth throughout the Bible's timeline.

- When the time came to free the Israelites from Egyptian slavery, God had already spent decades preparing Moses to lead.

- When it was time to navigate God's people through Egypt's famine, God had already spent years teaching humility and leadership skills to Joseph to preserve the people.

- When it came time to rebuild the walls around Jerusalem, God spent years grooming Nehemiah as cupbearer to Ahasuerus's son Artaxerxes, to be in the right position at the right time.

And when the decree was issued to annihilate His chosen people in Persia, God already had Esther in place.

God is never surprised by our situation or at a loss for prepared servants to perfectly meet those needs.

In this season of life, you may be the one in need or the one whom God has strategically placed to help others. Either way, when you look back and trace His fingerprints in your circumstances, you will find that He has been preparing you for it all along.

DAY 4
God's Providence

And they told Mordecai what Esther had said. Then
Mordecai told them to reply to Esther, "Do not think to
yourself that in the king's palace you will escape any more
than all the other Jews. For if you keep silent at this time,
relief and deliverance will rise for the Jews from another
place, but you and your father's house will perish. And
who knows whether you have not come to the kingdom
for such a time as this?"

(Esther 4:12–14)

During the course of leading the 2019 Holy Land tour, one of my long-time friends on the tour was teasing me about the combination of my maiden name, "Snow," and my married name, "Pyle." I'll admit, to be "Snow Pyle" *is* comical. Laughing, I told our tour guide, Ori, that I should change it back to Snow since I had been divorced nearly ten years. When I said that, he stopped, looked me straight in the eye with a puzzled expression, and asked why I chose to hang on to an identity that had been severed so long ago. Interestingly, I couldn't answer.

There was no malice or judgment in his question, only a candid moment of frank curiosity propelled by astonishment. But his momentary question caused me to ponder long and hard. My ex-husband and I had no children, so keeping his last name for the reason of continuity did not apply.

As I pondered and prayed while walking where Jesus walked, God helped me realize that somewhere deep inside I was still hanging on to the past instead of completely stepping into the future He'd prepared for me. I actually silently argued with God. *It's been ten years! I moved on a long time ago! A name doesn't really make a difference. So what that I haven't changed it?* And on and on it went. God finally led me to realize that I was embracing an argument instead of embracing a change. It was finally time to snip the final thread and be "me" once again.

Consequently, a month after returning home from the Holy Land (two days before Christmas), I filed a court petition to change my surname back to Snow. The reaction of my family and friends truly filled my heart with joy. The overwhelming response was *"Finally!"*

The judge signed the court order on February 13, 2020, officially changing my name back to Donna Michelle Snow. Then began the Herculean task of transitioning my name in the literary world, along with changing all of my IDs, cards, memberships, titles, deeds, and ministry DBA. Yes, it was quite a chore that took months. However, as each new ID arrived bearing "Snow," my heart danced. It is truly delightful to be "me" once again.

There comes a time in our lives when we need someone to remind us who we truly are. It may be a casual question such as Ori asked me. However, it often takes someone to speak a hard truth or ask a probing question in response to our choices. More often than not, those words come from someone who loves us and has our best interests at heart.

Can you remember a time when a relative or friend spoke strong words to you that changed your course of action in an important circumstance? If so, what happened?

So why all this talk about names and true identities? Simply this: Mordecai was about to get real with Esther about those very issues.

Read Esther 4:12–14.

In Esther's case, she heard a hard truth from her cousin Mordecai that was spoken out of love and concern. He sensed that Esther was giving in to fear. Even though their situation was dire, it must have been difficult for Mordecai. He found himself in the delicate position of speaking hard words to his cousin, not because he wanted to, but because circumstances dictated that he needed to.

In Esther 4:13–14, what three main points did Mordecai make?

1.

2.

3.

Basically, he tells Esther, "You're dead if you do and dead if you don't. Either way, there's no escape." He reminded her that identity matters. Perhaps he was reminding her without words, "Remember you are Hadassah, an Israelite daughter of God's covenant promise!" She answered to her Persian name "Esther," but that was not her true identity.

According to these verses, what is your identity in Christ?

John 1:12–13

1 Peter 2:9

Galatians 3:27–29

Ephesians 4:22–24

Receiving Jesus as Lord and Savior by faith means receiving a new identity. It does not mean that we lose ourselves; rather, we become who He created us to be, buried and raised to new life with Him. There is nothing greater than experiencing the fullness of union with Jesus. You are His daughter by faith and an heir to the promise!

Esther 4 contains the very heart and mission of the Book of Esther. Write the last sentence of Esther 4:14:

For such a time as this. These timeless, vital words remind us that you and I have a limited time on this earth. God chose you to be born to the parents you have, live in the area you live, exist in this particular generation, marry the spouse you have, bear the children you did, work in the job you work—everything God has planned for you intersects *for such a time as this.*

Where do you see God using you in specific ways today *for such a time as this?* Did you ever view it through that lens before?

where are you in the grocery store or in a season of a moment for a moment such this.

Even though Mordecai's words to Esther were harsh, they were spoken out of love, not law. He did not threaten to expose her. He merely stated that she would not escape the genocide when her heritage became known. Love, not law, moves hearts to be courageous. Jesus is our perfect example.

We have a choice when someone we love tells us necessary, hard truths: believe them or dismiss them. By God's grace, Esther believed Mordecai's words. We glimpse the providence of God here because Mordecai's words convey the unspoken belief that God will come through on His promise to deliver His people.

Mordecai's words forced Esther to pray, think, strategize, stand up, and ask others to stand with her, relying solely on God. Esther's courage, perhaps long masked by silence, was finally uncovered.

Has God ever put you in a position to lovingly speak hard, necessary truths to someone you love? How were your words received?

There have been a few times in my life when I felt that God had prompted me to talk with someone I love in such a manner. Each time, three things were true: (1) I had just been in His Word or prayer, so I felt the prompting came from Him; (2) I didn't want to speak to the person for fear that confrontation would harm our relationship; and (3) I prayed before and after I spoke with them, asking God to use those words to build up, not tear down.

Esther's female powers of face and form were not enough. Her desire to remain silent actually stood in her way. Esther's bravery is unmistakable as she takes the stand that liberating her people was far more important than remaining queen of Persia.

Esther had been mostly silent up to this point and content to live in the shadows following the dictates of others. Thanks to Mordecai speaking the truth in love, Esther finally steps forward into what God has prepared her for all along: to be instrumental in saving His chosen people.

By that step of faith, Esther becomes part of the solution and not part of the problem. She relinquished control of her own security and fear by turning control over to God.

Sometimes we ask if God is in control of the world.

Perhaps the deeper question is "Is God in control of my life?"

I am so thankful that God has chosen you to open the Book of Esther with this study for such a time as this. I pray that God continues to challenge, encourage, and inspire you to love and serve Him more deeply each day.

DAY 5
If I Perish, I Perish

Then Esther told them to reply to Mordecai, "Go, gather all the Jews to be found in Susa, and hold a fast on my behalf, and do not eat or drink for three days, night or day. I and my young women will also fast as you do. Then I will go to the king, though it is against the law, and if I perish, I perish." Mordecai then went away and did everything as Esther had ordered him.

(Esther 4:15–17)

A multiple-day fast is both challenging and transforming. I have done it only once in my life. I believed that God was leading me to start a Bible study writing and teaching ministry. That was a daunting thought because I didn't grow up in the church. So I undertook a three-day fast that began on Maundy Thursday after church and ended on Easter Sunday morning.

Since Good Friday is a work holiday, I simply stayed home. I spent that time praying, taking long walks with a journal and Bible, reading God's Word endlessly, and tinkering in the garden. I spent normal mealtimes in prayer about many things and many people. However, the main focus was to seek God's direction regarding whether or not to launch the ministry. That weekend, God led me to a resounding "yes," and now, over a decade later, He has proven faithful time and again.

Up to this point in the story, Esther has enjoyed mostly quiet seclusion from the drama happening outside the palace gates. Then Ahasuerus's decree completely shattered Esther's relative tranquility. The camera pans over to Mordecai mourning at the city gate over the king's decree. Mordecai cleverly finds a way to let Esther know what has transpired and speaks the truth in love to spur her to help *for such a time as this*. Today's lesson is pivotal in Esther's story as she emerges with a new determination and confident voice.

At long last, Esther is harkened back to her Jewish roots to step up as an unlikely heroine in God's rescue of His people.

Read Esther 4:15–17.

In contrast to Esther's mild demeanor until now, what change do you see in her?

Esther realizes that the problem far exceeds her capabilities, and she morphs from a quiet, meek girl into a purpose-filled woman who takes charge by seeking spiritual support. She tells Mordecai to fast for three solid days, along with all Persian Jews, and commands her attendants to fast along with her.

Have you experienced a time when you needed specific spiritual support to face a specific upcoming challenge? If so, what?

What was the result?

Esther 4:16 records the second time Esther speaks in our drama. What does she say?

Wow! We now see a much different Esther emerge from her voiceless cocoon. Look back at Esther 4:10–11. What is the difference between her stance in 4:10–11 and 4:16?

In Esther 4:16, Esther conveys strength and an unshakable faith. Mordecai reminded Esther of her roots and obligations to encourage her away from fear toward faith. At first, she balks, as many of us might. But Mordecai's words have struck a chord in Esther. No sooner does Mordecai finish speaking than Esther performs a 180-degree turn (in dainty slippers, of course).

What did Esther specifically ask Mordecai to do in 4:16?

Esther's request for an all-encompassing prayer for all Judeans reveals her compassion and selflessness.

Despite the absence of God's name, His fingerprints are all over Esther's humble request. She displays her authentic faith in God as she admits the need for faith-filled support to seek His intervention. Significantly, up to this point she has been silent about her Jewish roots. Now, she not only shares her true identity with her maidservants but also her faith as she enlists their support.

Although not specifically mentioned in Esther 4:3, prayer usually accompanied such fasting in Jewish tradition. In the following passages, identify who is fasting and praying and why:

Ezra 8:21–23

Joel 2:12

Luke 2:36–38

Acts 13:3

The whole point of fasting is to set your mind and heart on the Lord, which includes communicating with Him through prayer. One thing is crystal clear: by asking for such an elongated, diligent fast, Esther believes in the power of prayer, that God answers prayer, and that prayer can change her situation.

What do you believe about prayer?

When you and I pray, we call on the greatest power in existence to act. Yes, He already knows our thoughts, motives, and unspoken pleas, yet He invites us into an intimate relationship with Him through the regular conversation of prayer.

Esther asks Mordecai to fast, but that also inferred prayer. Fasting without praying would be like attending morning worship without singing or attending Bible study without opening a Bible.

Fasting is mentioned in both the Old and New Testaments and is most often connected to making a petition or request before God. So even though Esther mentions only fasting, prayer routinely accompanied it.

Fasting is not a spiritual discipline often mentioned in our day-to-day lives, but it was common among the Jews. Although they were required to fast only on the Day of Atonement, many other examples of fasting occur throughout Scripture.

What does Isaiah 58:1–12 say about fasting?

Fasting was often used to express sorrow or as a way to be humble before God. How did David humble himself in Psalm 35:13?

Fasting contains many spiritual benefits, but fasting can also be misinterpreted and used inappropriately. How?

What is your understanding of biblical fasting?

If you have ever fasted, what spiritual result did you discern?

In the New Testament, fasting served as a way to draw close to the Lord through focused meditation. In Matthew 4:1–2, who fasted, where, and for how long?

In Matthew 6:16–18, what does Jesus say about fasting?

I can barely keep my face from drooping when I can't indulge in chocolate cake. (I know, right?) My sadness is obvious to anyone within ten square miles. Obviously, a temporary chocolate inconvenience does not whatsoever qualify as fasting. Jesus was making the point that we do not fast to garner sympathy from others; rather, fasting is a spiritual discipline to help us focus on God.

The end of Esther 4:16 is one of the key phrases that immediately comes to mind when we think of the Book of Esther. Fill in the blanks:

"Then I will go to the king, though it is against the law,

and if I _____, **I** _____."

Again, wow! Have you ever uttered similar words and actually meant them? Millions of Christians around the globe are persecuted daily. They live that statement every single day through faith.

Esther's declaration marks the public moment when she commits her decision and the outcome to God. Though she may have inwardly been resolute before then, she steps out from behind the veil to make it known to all.

Another significant, yet easily missed, nuance in her words is that she was also taking an unspoken stand to break the law of obedience to her husband and monarch. She had just agreed to approach him uninvited and risk her very life.

Each of us reaches that pivotal moment in our faith walk where our faith is no longer dependent on our parents, spouse, or any other person. It's the time to stand up and proclaim what you believe to be true for you. For some, that happened at confirmation. For others, at their adult Baptism (like me).

When was that moment in your life?

How did God change you through that moment?

That moment made me more aware of the Rock on which I stand. Those moments can overflow with emotions such as confidence, hope, trepidation, and much more.

If you are still standing behind a veil (like Esther), how could you pray to come out from behind it?

Once again, there are similarities to Ruth's story and Esther's story. Like Ruth, Esther is a beautiful woman committed to God.

What does Ruth declare to her mother-in-law, Naomi, in Ruth 1:16?

That certainly sounds a whole lot like "If I perish, I perish." Both of these strong, courageous women submitted to a wiser authority and God's divine guidance. Consequently, God used them to accomplish great things. Each woman was instrumental in God's plan to bring our Savior into the world.

Jesus prayed in the Garden of Gethsemane the night before His crucifixion. He asked His three closest disciples to stay awake, to keep watch, and to pray with Him. They all failed. Imagine for a moment if Esther had asked for prayer and Mordecai and the others failed to support her.

In the Garden of Gethsemane, Jesus uttered the words mirrored in Esther. Write what Jesus says in Luke 22:42:

When it comes to wholeheartedly serving Christ, a prerequisite is laying down our life, picking up our cross, and following Him. I will not blow smoke up your sequined ball gown—it is not easy. Picking up our cross and following Him can be an arduous, strenuous journey. But we do not walk in our strength! As we pick up our cross, the faith-filled lips of believers echo Esther's words: "If I perish, I perish."

Once Esther utters those words, what does Mordecai do according to verse 17?

In that moment, the cousins reverse roles. Until that point, Esther has been on the receiving end of orders. Mordecai now takes instruction from Esther as she steps into the role that God has prepared her for all along.

Doing what the Lord has called us to step out and accomplish is more important than life on earth. Sometimes, it is easier to talk words than to take a stand.

As we reach the end of Lesson 4, take time to write here what you learned that can be applied to this season of your life. You are doing a fantastic job, sister! Walking through this study with you is an incredible privilege.

LESSON 5

High-Stakes Games

Esther 5

Esther has stepped into a position of authority, calling for a fast among all the Jews as she prepares to approach King Ahasuerus uninvited. She has not forgotten what happened to the last queen who crossed the king. She has Mordecai's undying support, along with that of all of her people, yet Esther had to act alone, trusting God to guide her footsteps. Just because God has providentially brought Esther to this influential point does not mean that life would be easy or untested. Esther's dilemma is our dilemma. Circumstances can hem us in and demand that we commit ourselves to exercise faith and act with courage. God's purposes far outweigh the difficulties of our circumstances. And now it was time for Esther to live that truth to save her people from genocide.

- **DAY 1**   Approaching the King *(Esther 5:1–2)*
- **DAY 2**   Keep Your Enemies Close *(Esther 5:3–5)*
- **DAY 3**   God's Perfect Timing *(Esther 5:6–8)*
- **DAY 4**   Malice Sabotages Joy *(Esther 5:9–13)*
- **DAY 5**   Bad Advice 101 *(Esther 5:14)*

KEY QUESTIONS

- What would you have asked for if half of the Persian Empire had been offered to you?
- If our King of kings could grant you any request, what would it be?

- What assurances do you have that when you ask God for something, it will be granted?

- Where do you find peace in the midst of life's turmoil?

- When someone offends or angers you, do you simmer and plan to get even?

DAY 1
Approaching the King

On the third day Esther put on her royal robes and stood in the inner court of the king's palace, in front of the king's quarters, while the king was sitting on his royal throne inside the throne room opposite the entrance to the palace. And when the king saw Queen Esther standing in the court, she won favor in his sight, and he held out to Esther the golden scepter that was in his hand. Then Esther approached and touched the tip of the scepter.

(Esther 5:1–2)

The first time I slipped on a formal dress was for my high school senior prom. Even though I was a tomboy from a young age, everything had to be pink. My bedroom walls, comforter, hairbrush—even my Huffy bicycle with handlebar streamers. So naturally, my first formal dress looked like a cone of pink cotton candy.

It was the eighties, so my hair was piled as tall as the Empire State Building and plastered in place with a whole can of hairspray. After all, that whole run-your-fingers-through-your-hair natural look wasn't in style until much later. My fingernails and toenails were pink, the corsage my date gave me was pink, and life was just peachy.

Aside from the whole pink spectacle, I remember one specific thing: I stood taller. Well, I was five feet nine inches, but that's not what I'm talking about. I *felt* taller. I walked more smoothly. I avoided rain puddles. It was almost like that dress expected more out of me than a routine evening. It was the first time I understood the phrase that the clothes make the man (or woman, in my case).

After studying four chapters of the Book of Esther, covering many years, the story's camera zooms in on a single, pivotal day. The time has come for Esther to approach the king. And the first thing she does is put on her royal robes.

Even though Mordecai and Esther have chosen to fight against Haman's evil genocide of the Persian Jews, we cannot forget that they themselves face destruction. They have witnessed the ambition, pride, and self-glorification of Haman in a culture that wholeheartedly embraced such traits.

We left off last lesson with Mordecai hearing Esther's plea for fasting and promptly going off and doing as Esther had ordered. The Apocrypha inserts two noncanonical additions into the timeline's narrative at this point: (1) a prayer from Mordecai, and (2) a prayer from Esther. Let's look at a few important quotes from each.

MORDECAI'S PRAYER

> You know all things; you know, O Lord, that it was not in insolence or pride or for any love of glory that I did this and refused to bow down to this proud Haman. For I would have been willing to kiss the soles of his feet, to save Israel! But I did this that I might not set the glory of man above the glory of God, and I will not bow down to anyone but you, my Lord; and I will not do these things in pride. And now, O Lord God and King, God of Abraham, spare your people; for they are looking to annihilate us, and they desire to destroy the inheritance that has been yours from the beginning. Do not neglect your portion, which you redeemed for yourself out of the land of Egypt. Hear my prayer and have mercy upon your allotment and turn our mourning into feasting, that we may live and sing praise to your name, O Lord; do not destroy the mouth of those who praise you.
>
> (Addition C, 13:12–17)[17]

What aspects of Mordecai's prayer do you find significant?

Why?

It is hard to miss the substantial references to God as Mordecai's prayer includes his commitment to and reliance on God. This is precisely why it is important to include the Apocryphal additions in our study. The additions "sought ways to improve upon the story by adding more material. They did this for a variety of reasons, such as making the story more clearly religious and answering questions about the activities and motives of persons in the story."[18]

In a book where God's name is absent, this text clearly shows that He was there all along. Mordecai was a man of prayer, which means that he was a man of God.

ESTHER'S PRAYER

> And Esther the queen, seized with deathly anxiety, fled to the Lord; she took off her splendid apparel and put on the garments of distress and mourning, and instead of costly perfumes she covered her head with ashes and dung, and she utterly humbled her body and every part that she loved to adorn she covered with her tangled hair. And she prayed to the Lord God of Israel and said: "O my Lord, you only are our King; help me, who am alone and have no helper but you, for my danger is in my hand. Ever since I was born I have heard in the tribe of my family that you, O Lord, took Israel out of all the nations and our fathers from among all their ancestors for an everlasting inheritance and that you did for them all that you promised. . . Put eloquent speech in my mouth before the lion and turn his heart to hate the man who is fighting against us, so that there may be an end of him and those who agree with him. But save us by your hand and help me, who am alone and have no helper but you, O Lord."
>
> (Addition C, 14:1–5, 13–14)[19]

What aspects of her prayer do you find significant? Why?

These apocryphal prayer additions provide insight into the spiritual struggles that Esther and Mordecai might have felt at the time. Scholars, including Luther, thought much the same since they have been preserved for us in the Apocrypha over the centuries. We cannot claim them as absolute fact since they reside outside of Scripture, but the additions help us visualize the spiritual battle that would otherwise be absent.

Now, let's dig into our text! Read Esther 5:1–2.

Showing respect to those in authority accomplishes much. What does Esther put on before she goes to meet Ahasuerus?

Esther properly prepared herself to meet the king. Her attire fit the pomp of the occasion. Though I have never met a sitting US President or the Queen of England, if I knew such a meeting was forthcoming, I would certainly take special care to prepare my appearance. Chances are you would too.

On which day did Esther put on her royal robes?

Numbers are significant and are assigned special meaning throughout Scripture. The number 3 denotes divine perfection and completeness. For instance, God finished the fundamental work of creating our earthly nursery in three days before filling it with life on the other three days. The number 3 also denotes resurrection, as in Christ's resurrection from the dead on the third day.

Esther, her maids, Mordecai, and all Persian Jews had just completed three days of fasting (and prayer), so it was time for Esther to make good on her promise, trusting God to lead the charge.

Even though she was dressed appropriately on the outside, how do you think Esther felt on the inside? She was walking into the king's chamber knowing that thousands of people had just spent three days asking God to give her the words and the strength needed. It must have been empowering and humbling in equal measure.

In the Garden of Gethsemane, Jesus did not have the benefit of the disciples' prayers with and for Him, but that didn't stop Him from doing what needed to be done.

Perhaps some Christians get the impression that if we implore enough people to pray for us, God will answer our prayers in the way that we ask. It certainly does not hurt to have the prayers of the saints, but God does not require it. And if what we are praying counters God's will, it will not come to pass anyway.

In Esther 5:1, where is the king sitting?

Positioned on his throne provides a clear indication that the king was holding court in his audience chamber. He was likely surrounded by courtiers, visitors, and many other people.

With such an audience, why didn't Esther expose Haman and his evil plot before the king right then?

God provides Esther with the wisdom to know that it was neither the right time nor the right place. She needs to approach the king with her request in a more private setting. The decree to kill the Jews had caused significant confusion and grief around the empire. Esther likely took that into consideration to avoid adding to the public drama.

In Esther 5:2, what did the king hold out to Esther?

The golden scepter! Look back at Esther 4:11. Why was the king's act meaningful?

The historian Herodotus records that access to the king was limited to noble families and similar "safe" people. Archaeologists have uncovered many Persian reliefs depicting the king holding a scepter as he held court.

As for a scepter, in Matthew 27:29–30, it is telling that in their mockery of Jesus, the Roman soldiers put a reed in His hands as His royal scepter, the symbol of His power and authority. And then they ripped it out of His hands and beat Him over the head with it.

A scepter could also be in view in Matthew 28:18 when the risen Jesus said, *"All authority in heaven and earth has been given to Me."* And on the basis of that authority, Jesus gave the Great Commission. In a sense, each time we pray, Christ extends His scepter to us, His bride.

Consequently, even though historical information as to accuracy of that Persian scepter practice is scarce, such a scenario as described in Esther is not out of the realm of possibility.

What did Esther do when the king extended the golden scepter?

The moment that Esther touched the end of the king's scepter, she immediately received the king's grace. She had received the gift to live.

The moment that we receive God's gift of faith to believe in Jesus Christ as our Lord and Savior, we immediately receive the King's grace. We re-

ceive the gift to live eternally with Him. **What does that truth stir inside of you?**

It may be odd, but it stirs a fresh perspective in me. Yes, it also stirs soul-deep gratitude and so much more heartfelt emotion. But that fresh perspective is confidence. Not confidence in myself. It's a confidence in Christ, that no matter what happens today, Jesus already knows it, has already worked out how to navigate me through it, and will walk right beside me every step of the way.

Christ-centered perspective makes us brave.

Esther bravely faced down a *very real* threat of death. Conversely, Haman suffered no real threat from the Jews—it was merely a perceived threat born out of hatred. There's an ocean of difference between a real enemy and a perceived enemy.

Have you ever had a real enemy, or were they merely perceived as an enemy? What kind of difficulty did they cause for you? Was a solution ever reached?

Sometimes, other factors can contribute to labeling someone as an enemy, such as our own ego, pride, and stubbornness. This is evident when Haman labeled Mordecai and the Jews as enemies. They were not advancing on him with weapons drawn. One Jew bruised his ego and how others perceived him, so Haman retaliated by ordering a kingdomwide massacre. Perhaps Haman would have benefited from learning the art of "appropriate response."

Sometimes, when we experience violence or the threat of violence, our earthly enemies can pose significant danger. But we have an ultimate enemy that threatens eternal danger: Satan. When we remember that we have a true enemy in Satan, it forces us to reassess our classification of our enemies. How have you reassessed this lately?

Oftentimes, we see the person in front of us as an enemy when the real enemy is lurking in the shadows around the corner laughing as he pulls puppet strings. What is Satan's goal for us according to the first half of John 10:10?

What is God's goal for us according to the second half of John 10:10?

God always has the final say.

Esther's bravery could rank her deeds among those faith giants in Hebrews 11. She called on Mordecai, all Judeans, and her attendants to fast, but she did not stop there. *She acted.* She demonstrated faith that God would work without assuming someone else would step up.

What does James 2:20 tell us?

Faith apart from deeds is dead. In other words, we can sit around all day and talk about the love of God, but we are called to go out into the world and actually demonstrate His love to others.

Ironically, Luther was not fond of that section of James in Scripture, especially when his opponents were referencing that very verse to contradict him. Perhaps over time he came to understand and agree with it. However, Luther demonstrated his faith through works by igniting the Protestant Reformation. Esther demonstrated her faith through works by igniting change.

How is your faith working in this season of life?

What does God promise in 2 Chronicles 7:14?

When we humble ourselves and work out our faith with trembling, trusting the Lord to act on His promises, and turn our face toward His, eternal change is possible in *every* heart and *every* circumstance.

We close today's study breathing a sigh of relief. The king was receptive to Esther's presence, which means he is receptive to her request. When you and I approach our heavenly King's throne of grace, we need never fear that we will be rejected.

In Christ, God extended to each of us a cross-shaped scepter. His all-encompassing grace is freely extended because Jesus has already paid the price to give us life. What a beautiful truth to think about as we close today's lesson.

DAY 2
Keep Your Enemies Close

> And the king said to her, "What is it, Queen Esther? What
> is your request? It shall be given you, even to the half of my
> kingdom." And Esther said, "If it please the king, let the
> king and Haman come today to a feast that I have prepared
> for the king." Then the king said, "Bring Haman quickly,
> so that we may do as Esther has asked." So the king and
> Haman came to the feast that Esther had prepared.
>
> (Esther 5:3–5)

The camera lights return to the king's court to find Esther in royal robes, accepting the king's scepter and given the opportunity to speak. Imagine that scene. It was likely rare for the queen to be seen in public, much less in the king's court. All eyes swivel as her beautiful form and robes sweep into the throne room and she stands facing the king.

Read Esther 5:3–5.

Following strict protocol, Esther waits for Ahasuerus to initiate the conversation. What does he ask her in verse 3?

And what does he promise her?

Notably, this is the first time that the king actually addresses Esther as "Queen Esther." Perhaps it was because they were in his court chamber. Perhaps it was because she was dressed in her royal finery. Whatever the reason, the king feels obliged to finally address her as such, which can only play in her favor.

As for the king's promise, how many of us would have been tempted to request personal benefits or wealth? What would you have requested if the king had asked you that question?

Many of us may have treated it like Aladdin's lamp. However, the phrase "even to the half of my kingdom" was a royal catchphrase of promise. It wasn't intended to be taken literally. This phrase appears in the New Testament as well.

In what situations does that phrase appear in Mark 6:21–25?

Even though what she requested is morbid, Herodias's daughter did not request half of the kingdom. Rather than saying to Esther that he will actually divide his kingdom, Ahasuerus is simply conveying his willingness to be generous.

This was her moment! Esther could remind the king about the genocidal decree, expose Haman, and ask for her people to be spared. But that's not what happens. The author now records the third time Esther speaks.

What does she say in 5:4?

Esther pauses. She can't say it. Even though her request to save her people was right, the timing was wrong. In that moment, we once again see God's providence as He gives Esther the spiritual discernment to wait. And it makes all the difference in this dramatic story.

Imagine that you are standing before God, our heavenly King, and He asks: *What is your request?* How would you respond? Even though God says that He will prepare a feast of rich foods for us in heaven (Isaiah 25:6), that is probably not your request today. Right now, today, in this season of life, what lays heavy on your heart?

Pause here to spend some time in prayer, laying that request before God.

Esther paused, as well, but instead of asking for protection and rescue of her people, she invited the king and her archenemy to a banquet. *What?* Esther stood tall and did not flinch as she made her request. The man who instigated the decree of death against the Jews has just been invited to dinner. Her actions convey loud and clear that she trusts God to protect her and her people.

When it comes to Jewish people exhibiting such courage in the face of doom, my mind immediately pictures the Holocaust. The word *holocaust* has two entirely different meanings in secular and religious realms. According to the Oxford Dictionary of the Christian Church, *holocaust* means a sacrifice completely consumed by fire and thus a perfect sacrifice. The word *holocaust* translated several times in the Old Testament references animal sacrifices (Numbers 28:3; 29:2; Leviticus 1:3; 9:2).

However, since the 1950s, the word *holocaust* came to be applied to the Nazi persecution of Jews due to their practice of "completely consuming" the victims in mass gas chambers.

The similarities between Haman and Hitler are eerie. Their outer facade championed manners, while the inner truth championed massacre. In 1938, the Nazis released an official poster of Adolph Hitler. Under his stern, larger-than-life image, read the untruthful words of unity: *Ein Volk, ein Reich, ein Führer!* Translated, it means "One people, one empire, one leader."

What was intentionally left out of Hitler's poster was that the destruction of the many would be the means to reach his goal. History reveals that

Haman and Hitler were influenced by Satan. They sought to destroy the children of God's promise and, along with it, the promised Savior of the world (Genesis 12:3; 24:7; Galatians 3:16).

By His grace alone, what does God promise in Psalm 91:14?

Sin in our hearts causes destruction through hatred, carnage, and holocaust. Yet God made us in His image, regardless of race, ethnicity, or any other difference. In Romans 9:3–4, Paul wrote that the Jews were his *"kinsmen according to the flesh. They are Israelites, and to them belong the adoption, the glory, the covenants, the giving of the Law, the worship, and the promises."* Harboring hatred or malice, whether Jew or Gentile, is a sin.

Jesus, the Son of a virgin Jewish mother, died for *all* people according to God's perfect plan. In John 4:22, Jesus reminds us that *"salvation is from the Jews."*

It has been said over the course of history that you should keep your friends close, but keep your enemies closer. This is exactly what Esther did. She invited her mortal enemy for a congenial banquet. In that moment, we picture Jesus sitting at the table with Judas, who price-tagged Jesus at thirty pieces of silver.

When you and I approach God our heavenly King, He does not extend to us half of His kingdom. He offers us the entire kingdom, because His Son's death opened wide the gates of heaven for all who believe.

DAY 3
God's Perfect Timing

> And as they were drinking wine after the feast, the king
> said to Esther, "What is your wish? It shall be granted you.
> And what is your request? Even to the half of my kingdom,
> and it shall be fulfilled." Then Esther answered, "My wish
> and my request is: If I have found favor in the sight of the
> king, and if it please the king to grant my wish and fulfill
> my request, let the king and Haman come to the feast that
> I will prepare for them, and tomorrow I will do as the king
> has said."
>
> (Esther 5:6–8)

Have you ever experienced a moment when you have mentally prepared yourself to say something important or ask a burning question, only to find yourself hesitating? Welcome to Esther's current situation. She risked her life to approach Ahasuerus uninvited only to ask him to dinner. *Oh, and bring your friend Haman.*

The curtain opens to Esther's beautiful table and remains of an elaborate feast. The king and Haman have finished their meal, and now the wine is flowing.

Read Esther 5:6–8.

Herodotus wrote more than once how the Persian royalty loved turning banquets into sumptuous shindigs. He recorded feasts that included whole cooked animals (such as ostrich and ox) to ornate desserts and, of course, vast quantities of wine. Interestingly, he noted that these affairs tended to be dignified rather than boisterous. The Persian culture did not esteem or encourage gluttony or excess to the point of becoming sick.

So even though Esther's banquet for the king and Haman was likely lavish, it was orderly. Now if marriage reinforces anything, it is this truth: "A way to a man's heart is through his stomach." Esther had been Ahasuerus's wife for half a decade. She understood this truth, as well. She knew that any request that she made to the king would fare a much better chance of being granted if his stomach was full of fine food and fine wine.

So after the meal was over and the gentlemen held glasses of wine, what does Ahasuerus ask Esther in 5:6?

It is almost verbatim to what the king asked in 5:3, with one important exception: Ahasuerus does not address Esther by name *or* title. This may speak to how comfortable he felt in her presence. After all, as far as the story goes, she has created no difficulties whatsoever for Ahasuerus. So without preamble, the king simply jumps straight to the point.

How could her relaxed, home-court advantage play in Esther's favor?

The author now records the fourth time Esther speaks. How does she respond to the king in 5:7?

Esther had the king right where she needed him! The king was unencumbered by an entourage, relaxed, and receptive after enjoying a sumptuous meal and marinating his throat with wine. Conditions were prime to turn the king's favor from Haman to Mordecai. So why does Esther hesitate?

We can only ponder the reasons why Esther delayed her request to Ahasuerus since the text is silent. However, since God's providence is evident throughout the Book of Esther, we recognize this God-ordained pause. *Just wait.*

Do you struggle with waiting on God's timing? If so, when?

Waiting on God's timing inevitably causes us to exhale long, repent wholeheartedly, surrender impatience, and be still—even though we may want to move ahead like a bull in a china shop.

What do the following verses say about patience and God's timing?
2 Peter 3:8–9

[handwritten: God determines our steps]

Proverbs 16:9

[handwritten: 1 day is like 1,000 years]

I keep those words from Proverbs close, because as a bona fide organizer, boy howdy do I love planning my steps! Planning and organizing are my forte. Can you relate? *Please tell me you can so I don't feel alone.*

I have been a legal secretary going on thirty years. I have had *decades* of practice. I can organize your entire life in an afternoon. As a writer, I love journals, the art of writing, school supplies, and making lists. As a gardener, I love planning which vegetables to plant at which time of the year and when to start the seeds for each. You name it. I love anything that lets me use my love of planning and organization. *[handwritten: Blake]*

Well, being such a gung ho planner and organizer has often left me lacking sensitivity to waiting on God's timing. To exercise patience when God puts us in a holding pattern is a sign of a mature faith. Impatience provides the opportunity to repent and pray. *[handwritten: repent? pray-yes]*

How do you combat impatient moments if you experience them?

[handwritten: Spirit Book]

[handwritten: To discuss guilt or recognize where]

[handwritten margin note top: why call him enemy if we are one only than to recognize we judge other as enemy]

Once again, we have to admire Esther's courage in the face of her ene-my. The king seemed clueless as to the empirewide drama that his decree had caused, much less the deep-seated animosity between Haman and the Jews. Yet Esther sits poised and relaxed, not rushing the moments, but pay-ing attention to each one.

As you see Esther's restraint, what can you learn from her tact and diplo-macy?

[handwritten: we not look at how we define ourselves? remorse a way of looking at things. yet they are a mirror image of ourselves, can we define others as guilt]

Esther had clearly used her time in the palace very well. She learned to play the cat and mouse game of give-and-take.

If Esther had been more concerned with her timeline than with God's, this story would have ended much differently.

More time needed to pass for Haman's unwise self-confidence to ripen.

If you struggle with impatience or waiting on God's timing, I'm right there with you, sister. Before you close the book on this lesson, spend some time in prayer asking God to mature that fruit in you.

[handwritten: as they are as opportunities to see things differently? To see & them as ourselves if only looking beyond what we see with the eyes of humanity, but see beyond our enemy's face looking instead into their soul? Here is another cliche but look into the ? to see beyond the judgment we could make, some times we see only strength comes from...]

167

DAY 4
Malice Sabotages Joy

And Haman went out that day joyful and glad of heart. But when Haman saw Mordecai in the king's gate, that he neither rose nor trembled before him, he was filled with wrath against Mordecai. Nevertheless, Haman restrained himself and went home, and he sent and brought his friends and his wife Zeresh. And Haman recounted to them the splendor of his riches, the number of his sons, all the promotions with which the king had honored him, and how he had advanced him above the officials and the servants of the king. Then Haman said, "Even Queen Esther let no one but me come with the king to the feast she prepared. And tomorrow also I am invited by her together with the king. Yet all this is worth nothing to me, so long as I see Mordecai the Jew sitting at the king's gate."

(Esther 5:9–13)

Esther's first banquet comes to a close, and Haman is riding high on a cloud of self-important exclusivity. After all, he had just enjoyed an intimate meal with only the king and queen present. But what is true of clouds is also true about happiness: dissipation happens.

Read Esther 5:9–13.

Just when you think Haman's ego couldn't inflate any larger, we are reminded of just how much space is still available in his ego balloon. As he leaves Esther's banquet to go home, Haman spies Mordecai.

How does he react when he sees Mordecai at the king's gate?

Haman was *filled with wrath*. In the original Hebrew, the word *wrath* (חמה, *chemah*) is the same word used to describe Ahasuerus's anger when

Vashti refused to answer his summons. It is a strong word often used in the Old Testament to describe God's wrath or fury (Deuteronomy 9:19; Psalm 6:1; Lamentations 4:11). The crucial difference here is that Haman's anger is not a righteous anger.

After he left his first private banquet with Ahasuerus and Esther, Haman is ecstatic about his privileged position, until his eyes fall on Mordecai standing at the gate. You can almost hear the bile gurgling in Haman's throat as he stomps by.

Haman's happiness lasts from moment to moment because it is based on circumstances. He's only happy when everything is going his way. Worldly happiness does not last. We know that. We've experienced it.

How would you define happiness?

Webster's defines it as a state of well-being and contentment based on a pleasurable or satisfying experience. Happiness is momentary. If you prefer the sun and it starts to rain, your happiness quotient would land in a puddle. Happiness is based on circumstances that are most often beyond our control.

We can rely on all of God's promises in Scripture, but happiness is not among them. Life is not fair. If it were, we would all be hell-bound, and Jesus would have never been crucified to redeem us. Jesus never promised us happiness. He promised that we would have trouble, but that He would overcome it (John 16:33).

On the other hand, how would you define joy?

According to Galatians 5:22–23, joy is a fruit of the Spirit. Joy comes from God and is His gift to us. We can certainly ask God for joy, but He's

169

all the answers don't have b there but the understanding that love at the end

already given it to us. Joy is a contentment that sees past our circumstances to God's promises of new life ahead. *(is all there is)*

Peace is also a fruit of the Spirit. It is a peace based on your salvation through faith, knowing that your sins have been forgiven. I have made some pretty big blunders in my life. I can spend my life beating myself up with guilt, or I can receive God's forgiveness, which brings peace.

that is all that is required for me to accept

Happiness is based on today; joy is based on eternity. *real joy only*

Haman's happiness fled because of one man's actions. That just goes to show you how influential one person can be in our life. It also clearly demonstrates that Haman did not possess the joy of the Lord.

If history has taught us anything, it is that overconfidence leads to downfall. Esther likely realized that as long as Haman felt overconfident about his position and forthcoming plans, he would eventually step into his own trap. Haman was confident that his star was on the rise, when in reality he was fewer than twenty-four hours from his fatal fall.

So Haman ignored Mordecai as he passed by the gate. Despite a blissful first banquet, what did Haman tell his wife and friends in Esther 5:11 once he returned home?

Patience is a gift of the spirit.

How many times in that one verse does "his" or "him" appear?

Haman could not see past his own nose to grasp the larger picture. His focus was on *himself* and what *he* had done, what *he* had received, and how *he* had been honored. He gave no glory to God or even Ahasuerus for those blessings. In his mind, he had achieved all of it through his own cunning and strength.

As a quick refresher, according to Esther 3:1, what was Haman's lineage?

Interestingly, the Septuagint (the Greek translation of the original He-brew) translates the word *Agagite* as "bully." Doesn't that add some insight into Haman's gene pool?

When self-centered, egotistical people become angry, they often stoop to bullying, intimidation, and threats to manipulate circumstances. How do you see this behavior in Haman?

We often struggle with injustice when the wicked seem to prosper at the expense of the righteous. The psalmist was no different.

In Psalm 73:12–13, what is the psalmist's struggle?

There are many areas of life in which I long to see justice against the wicked carried out. In my anti-trafficking volunteer work with Love146, it breaks my heart to see children exploited and trafficked while the perpetra-tors evade capture or prosecution for months or years as they harm even more children. But justice does not belong to us.

What does Romans 8:33–34 tell us?

Have you ever faced an injustice in your life? How did you respond?

When I have faced injustice, my first response is usually along the lines of "That isn't fair!" According to the following verses, how are Christ followers encouraged to respond to injustice?
Isaiah 1:17

Micah 6:8

When we see corruption, fighting, and self-directed agendas hurt the innocent, we long to see justice. We need only to remember the politically fueled riots and COVID-19 confusion across the United States during 2020. We long to be part of the solution to make our society more stable for all. Well, a stable society was far down Haman's agenda, if it appeared at all. Such circumstances must have been disheartening for both Mordecai and Esther.

As Haman walks through the streets past Mordecai, we see once again dark storm clouds brewing over Susa. But there is one bright spot: Mordecai still stands resolute.

Mordecai's godly bravery reminds us that as long as there is at least one person who risks his or her life to stand against injustice, God can take down any wicked person and break through a repressive society.

DAY 5
Bad Advice 101

Then his wife Zeresh and all his friends said to him, "Let a gallows fifty cubits high be made, and in the morning tell the king to have Mordecai hanged upon it. Then go joyfully with the king to the feast." This idea pleased Haman, and he had the gallows made.

(Esther 5:14)

Once again, in today's lesson the stage lights narrow to illuminate one verse. Esther's first banquet has happened. She invites Ahasuerus and Haman for round 2, her next banquet. Haman leaves full of self-importance at being included a second time in the king's private circle. Then he sees an unbowing Mordecai at the city gate. Haman rushes home to whine to his wife and friends about how disrespected he feels. Haman is about to learn that unless you want people to give you advice, don't tell them your problem.

Read Esther 5:14.

What stands out to you?

Haman's family and friends are just as vengeful and bloodthirsty as he is! Haman is so worked up about Mordecai that he does not stop to sift their suggestion through wisdom's filter.

Have you ever received bad advice from a family member or friend? What happened?

How did it affect your relationship with that person(s)?

Bad advice from friends and family can have devastating consequences. It can tear families apart so far that they never speak again. I can only imagine how that breaks the heart of God.

Haman pours out his self-centered woes to his wife and friends, and they come back with the worst advice possible: build gallows. Did anyone else have to pick up their jaw from the carpet after reading their response? They didn't even skip a beat. They suggested how high it should be and when the deed should be done. Talk about horrible advice!

Up until that suggestion, the author gives no hint that Haman had even considered the possibility of Mordecai's personal execution. His attention has been focused on wiping out all Jews, thereby including Mordecai automatically. But when this bad advice is cast, Haman takes the bait—hook, line, and sinker. Not every day do we witness the evil villain gathering enough rope to hang himself.

Haman progressed from being satisfied that Mordecai was included in the empirewide extermination pool to a bloodthirsty revenge of personally arranging Mordecai's execution.

What do the following verses say will happen to such people?
Psalm 7:14–16

Proverbs 5:22–23

Evil gives birth to lies, and mischief causes violence to fall on their own head. There should be a picture of Haman next to those verses.

Haman had become preoccupied, even obsessed, with Mordecai. His happiness was filtered through Mordecai's actions. His rage was aimed like darts at the face of Mordecai glued to a target.

Years ago, I worked with someone who lived for drama. If there wasn't any drama happening in the office, she would create some, sit back, and enjoy the show. Even on days when everything should have been smooth sailing, she would invent something to complain about, a procedure that was "woefully" inadequate, or point out a fellow employee who just didn't seem to be pulling their weight. You name it, she thought of it, and it was a new drama each week. Sometimes, each day. It got to where I loathed seeing her coming down the hall.

After about six months of working with the drama queen, a friend of mine asked why I was so tense. When I asked what she meant, she said that if I sensed any discord or disharmony in any situation, no matter how great or small, I would overreact. And by overreact, she meant that I would interrupt someone who was sharing a complaint and try to change the subject. If the subject would not return to happy topics, I would find a reason to leave the room.

I argued with her at first. *I have never acted like that, I thought.* Then I asked my family. They had noticed it too. I began praying for God to show me the root of my sudden intolerance for discord and disharmony. Needless to say, all roads pointed to my melodramatic co-worker. In that moment, it was like a lightbulb went off. From that day on, I gave that co-worker a wide berth rather than become embroiled in her self-created dramas. When she came to me with a complaint or issue, I would nod and smile and simply go about my day without taking any action.

God showed me that I was reacting rather than restraining. I was allowing myself to enter the drama instead of listening with discernment while considering the trustworthiness of the information source. Interestingly, when she realized that I no longer lunged for her drama bait, she stopped coming to me with the fishing pole. I learned to get along with her, but we were never destined to become best friends. And I had to stop being judge and jury regarding her actions. (Yes, I had nicknamed her "Drama Llama.") She answered to a higher authority than me, so over time God helped me simply put her drama in His hands.

Have you ever been preoccupied or obsessed about one person's toxic or harmful actions or simply their presence? If so, what was the initial cause?

What happened?

When we appoint ourselves judge and jury, the story never ends well. The wound festers until we surrender those feelings to the Lord. It may take a long time. Trust me, I know. However, as a deterrent to such behavior and for good reason to change, we need only look at Haman and every other egotistical person of power in Scripture.

As we close out Lesson 5, there is an undercurrent of emotion much darker here than Haman's unhappiness: *malice*. Webster's defines malice as evil intent on the part of a person who commits a wrongful act injurious to others. Malice possesses a long memory and never forgives. There is no peace when malice reigns.

Haman's deep-seated hatred of Mordecai is turning even darker.

We hear the pounding of the gallows-makers offstage.

The thunder begins to roll above.

The coffin-maker picks out a box.

Haman just does not realize that it will be sized for him.

LESSON 6

Guess Who's Coming to Dinner?

Esther 6–7

As Esther prepares for the sequel banquet for Ahasuerus and Haman, the king experiences insomnia. But God's providence is once again crystal clear as the king's insomnia allows him to rediscover how Mordecai saved his life. As the king can't sleep, Haman builds gallows for Mordecai. God brings Mordecai to their minds, yet for vastly different purposes. As the king seeks to honor Mordecai, Haman seeks to hang him. Esther's banquet sets the scene in motion.

- **DAY 1**   The King's Insomnia *(Esther 6:1–2)*
- **DAY 2**   Honoring a Hero *(Esther 6:3–11)*
- **DAY 3**   Impending Doom *(Esther 6:12–14)*
- **DAY 4**   Evil Unmasked *(Esther 7:1–6)*
- **DAY 5**   Victory over the Enemy *(Esther 7:7–10)*

KEY QUESTIONS

- Would you have handled Esther's situation differently? How?
- Do you patiently await God's perfect timing?
- When have you last stepped out in faith as Esther did? What was at stake?
- What enemy threatens you at this time?
- What lessons do Haman's actions teach you?

DAY 1
The King's Insomnia

On that night the king could not sleep. And he gave orders
to bring the book of memorable deeds, the chronicles, and
they were read before the king. And it was found written
how Mordecai had told about Bigthana and Teresh, two of
the king's eunuchs, who guarded the threshold, and who
had sought to lay hands on King Ahasuerus.

(Esther 6:1–2)

While it seemed like the whole world was sound asleep, I sat on the
floor surrounded by clothes from my chest of drawers. Once again, it was
2:00 a.m., and I was wide awake. Significant life changes were happening in
that season, and sleep dodged me like an Olympic slalom skier. So, naturally, I spent the wee hours organizing drawers, closets, and shelves.

You name it, I organized it, all between the hours of 10:00 p.m. and
2:30 a.m. for several weeks in a row. By the time life settled down again and
I began sleeping regularly, my house could have rivaled a Martha Stewart
organization makeover.

Neither music, reading, nor hot baths helped sleep come. I had to be
organizing something, even if it was just the silverware drawers (which
looked spectacular when I finished them, incidentally). Looking back over
that time, I realized that those organizational nights helped me feel as if I
had control over my life, which was far from the truth during normal business hours.

As the curtain opens on Esther 6, the king's bedchamber comes into
focus. He is tossing and turning. Insomnia seems odd considering the fact
that he just enjoyed Esther's excellent feast and wine earlier that evening.
Sleep should have come easily, but God had other plans.

Read Esther 6:1–2.

What did the king ask to be done to help him sleep?

Ahasuerus could have chosen any distraction to induce sleep. He had a queen and a harem full of beautiful women. He could have even counted sheep, yet he chose a book. Many people choose reading to lull them to sleep. However, the king did not choose a gripping novel or soothing bedtime rhymes. Instead, he chose from the books that chronicled his royal reign. If anything would induce sleep, it would be a book of deeds and chronicles. Unless the writer was gifted at weaving a captivating story, those entries must have been as dry as sheetrock.

If you have experienced insomnia, what helped you fall asleep again?

If you read, what do you choose?

I keep a few books by my bed in case insomnia strikes, but they are novels that draw my mind to lands faraway, not the Book of 1 Chronicles.

Insomnia can be frustrating, but there is a power greater in motion besides the servant's feet as he fetched a book from the king's from dusty shelves. What are the first five words of Esther 6:2?

And it was found written. Imagine for a moment how many books lined the king's shelves. He had been ruling over 127 provinces as Persia's king for years, and records were kept for all. Royal records preceded him all the way back to his father's and grandfather's reigns.

Yet his servant chose the *exact volume* that contained Mordecai's act of heroism. Then the servant turned to the *exact story* in the book of how Mordecai saved the king's life. This is one of the most compelling moments of God's divine providence in the entire Book of Esther.

God often uses the incidents that you and I consider insignificant to bring about the most significant changes. *Like a sleepless night.* He works all things together for good, and before we know it, we are on our face before Him in worship-filled awe over what He has accomplished.

In Esther 6:2, what story does the servant tell the king?

It was unusual for a king to overlook rewarding a person for special services to the crown, much less to completely forget about it. Mordecai's heroic act was a big one to forget. He had saved the king's life!

Let's pause for a moment to glance at what is not written here. Did you notice that Mordecai had never reminded the king about his heroic act? Mordecai simply did his duty by uncovering the assassination plot, reported the incident through Esther, and promptly returned to his duties at the gate.

Noticing Mordecai's humbleness here opens the door for us to notice similar instances elsewhere in our story. Even though his cousin was queen, Mordecai did not leverage Esther's position to benefit himself in any way. Although significant blessings are bestowed on Mordecai later in our story, they were not given because Mordecai demanded them out of sense of family entitlement.

Have you ever performed a significant act for someone who never acknowledged it or you? If so, what was it? What happened in the end?

If your act cost much time, talent, or treasure, it would be easy to hold hard feelings against that person. On the other hand, humility readily extends grace and forgiveness. The apostle Paul is someone from whom we can learn godly humility.

He provides an impressive list of his credentials in Philippians 3:4–6, but then what does he say in verses 7–8?

All earthly things are worthless compared to the surpassing greatness of knowing Christ. Paul could have taught a master class on humility. However, our greatest example of humility is Christ Himself. He left the splendors of heaven to be born to poor parents in a cattle trough.

What did Christ do for us according to Philippians 2:5–8?

How did God reward Jesus's humble sacrifice according to Philippians 2:9–11?

What do those words stir inside of you?

In a word, *gratitude.* You and I will never be able to repay the debt that Jesus's sacrifice erased on our behalf, and He doesn't ask for repayment. Instead, He invites us to join Him in eternity through faith. Joy!

The king's insomnia providentially triggers a change in the genocide tide. Until that point, the tide steadily rose against the Jews. But a Jew had now saved the king's life. The tides of change are on the horizon.

The same invisible hand that kept the king's eyelids open is the same hand that chose that particular book from among countless volumes. No detail, however small or insignificant, escapes God's mighty gaze. His is the same divine hand that guides every moment of every day. He works *all* things for our good and His glory.

So, if you are experiencing a bit of insomnia, ask God to lull you back to sleep with these hope-filled words:

Now I lay me down to sleep,

I pray the Lord my soul to keep.

If I should die before I rise,

Jesus' loving arms shall be my prize.

DAY 2
Honoring a Hero

And Haman said to the king, "For the man whom the king delights to honor, let royal robes be brought, which the king has worn, and the horse that the king has ridden, and on whose head a royal crown is set. And let the robes and the horse be handed over to one of the king's most noble officials. Let them dress the man whom the king delights to honor, and let them lead him on the horse through the square of the city, proclaiming before him: 'Thus shall it be done to the man whom the king delights to honor.'"

(Esther 6:7–9)

Viola Schultz was a woman of few words. Although retired, she was a woman on a mission. She lived within walking distance of church, and if the church doors were open, Viola was there.

She was one of the first women I met at church not long after I became a Christian in my early twenties. God led me to become involved in our church's chapter of the Lutheran Women's Missionary League, and Viola served as its president. She was diligent and kind, certainly not one to gravitate toward the spotlight. She was entirely content serving behind the scenes. Whether it was making coffee for Bible class on Sunday mornings, crocheting crosses for church Baptism gifts, or sewing quilts for Lutheran World Relief, she was truly a woman after God's own heart.

Viola took me under her wing when I joined the women's mission group and taught me more than I can ever share in a lifetime. Viola also taught me how to crochet those Baptism crosses. She believed every young lady should have proper homemaking skills, so she offered a free class at church to teach the next generation how to crochet.

Viola passed away peacefully in her sleep one evening. The church overflowed with mourners. Over and over, people commented on her humility. Through her humble service, she reflected God's kindness to thousands during her lifetime. I still miss her sweet smile.

From the back pew, Viola's servant heart and humble nature showed many the heart of God. In stark contrast, Haman's ego could rival the tower of Babel's architect. He believed that the spotlight should center on him, and he lived life accordingly.

Read Esther 6:3–11.

The old saying that the early bird gets the worm proves ironic in these passages. Haman arrived early to ensure an audience with the king. He likely stayed up all night supervising construction of the gallows. One of the most vivid reversals of fortune in the Book of Esther happens right here.

What does Haman assume from the king's words?

We see Haman's ego again strutting proud like a peacock. Naturally, Haman assumes that if anyone deserves to be honored, it should be he. Perhaps Haman's assumptions were inspired by the location where this conversation took place. Haman already enjoys unimpeded access to the king's court chamber as prime minister; now he is invited straight into the king's bedchamber! It was an exceedingly rare honor, so Haman reasoned that such honors should logically extend to a parade in his honor.

This drama's villain is a piece of work. He is proud, self-important, and self-aggrandizing. What do the following verses say about those traits?

Proverbs 15:25

Proverbs 16:5

Isaiah 2:11–12

In light of those verses, how does God view the sin of pride?

Do you struggle with pride? In what situation does it most often arise?

Pride can rear its ugly head in many ways. Pride in knowledge. Pride in a resume. Pride in parenting. Pride in accomplishments. Pride in position. Pride in wealth. Pride in beauty. Pride in rule keeping. Pride in a denomination. Even pride in humility. But God despises a proud spirit and will bring low all who find their worth in pride.

When we decide to take matters into our own hands as Haman did, it reveals a trust issue in our faith life. Haman was constantly working angles to advance rather than letting his actions earn merit. I have certainly been guilty of that, as well. Trusting God with what we consider "small" things can pose the biggest challenge.

After Haman filled the king's ears with what should be done to a man whom the king delights to honor, what does Ahasuerus say in Esther 6:10?

I wish photography had been invented to snap a picture at that moment. Can you imagine the look on Haman's face? I wonder how many shades of red his complexion deepened. Haman's blood must have been boiling, but he could hardly let the king see it. Blinded by his own pride and arrogance, Haman experiences a humiliating reversal of fortune. After expecting the spotlight to shine on him, he now has to carry it to illuminate Mordecai.

How does Ahasuerus identify Mordecai in Esther 6:10?

The king specifically labeled Mordecai as a Jew, a fact he likely learned for the first time as his servant read to him from the Chronicles. Clearly, Ahasuerus had completely forgotten that he granted Haman permission to destroy all of the Persian Jews, of which Mordecai was one.

What did Haman do for Mordecai in Esther 6:11?

Imagine being a citizen in Susa and witnessing Haman parading Mordecai through the streets in tribute. Talk about mixed messages! Mordecai was being honored by the very man who drafted the Jews' death decree. The king was simply repaying a debt to Mordecai for saving his life, not easing the people's fears about their impending genocide.

The irony cannot be overlooked. Mordecai refused to bow before Haman, yet now Haman leads Mordecai through the streets on horseback, proclaiming Mordecai's praises. God has a deliciously wonderful sense of humor.

Haman's morning had begun with an early visit to the king's chamber to ensure that Mordecai would be hanged on the gallows he had just built. Little did he know that the king's insomnia had effectively written Haman's death warrant.

As we close today's lesson, spend time pondering whether or not you struggle with pride. If so, spend time in prayer asking God to remove that sin from your life. If you struggle being humble, ask God to begin working humility into your life. Jesus is our perfect example.

DAY 3
Impending Doom

Then Mordecai returned to the king's gate. But Haman
hurried to his house, mourning and with his head covered.
And Haman told his wife Zeresh and all his friends everything that had happened to him. Then his wise men and
his wife Zeresh said to him, "If Mordecai, before whom
you have begun to fall, is of the Jewish people, you will
not overcome him but will surely fall before him." While
they were yet talking with him, the king's eunuchs arrived
and hurried to bring Haman to the feast that Esther had
prepared.

(Esther 6:12–14)

Michael was a heartthrob when it came to this teenage girl's feelings. I
was a high school sophomore, he was a junior, and I fell head over heels in
love as much as a girl possibly can at age 16. We both played in the band,
so that meant I could see him at after-school marching practice, music
rehearsals, football games, and pep rallies. Every time he walked into the
band hall, I would get those huge puppy eyes and melt. I just knew we were
going to get married one day. He, on the other hand, classified me as great
"friend" material. Unfortunately, I was too gooey-eyed to see it.

Several band kids usually gathered in the band hall each morning before classes just to hang out. One particular morning, Michael had already
left for class but had left his letterman jacket behind. A mutual friend ran
up and told me that Michael asked me to hang on to it for him so that it did
not disappear. Naturally, I assumed this meant that he was asking me to "go
steady." (Can you already see the disaster coming?) Instead of hanging his
jacket in a safe place, I wore it the entire school day like a promise ring. I
would blush each time someone asked who gave me his jacket. After all, I
had been *chosen,* you know.

Word raced like wildfire through the school until it finally reached Michael, who approached me warily at after-school rehearsal. As he walked
up to me, I just knew he would proclaim his undying love while imaginary

birds sang a background chorus. Kindly, but firmly, he said that he thought I was very nice and funny, but that we were just friends. Then he asked for his jacket back. I vaguely remember blushing magenta, apologizing profusely without looking him in the eye, and rushing home in a dramatic flood of tears. But the worst part of that whole ordeal was going to school the next morning to face all those kids without Michael's letterman jacket draped around me. Frankly, high school and hormones should happen decades apart.

As embarrassed as I was showing up at school without Michael's letterman jacket, it does not hold a torch to how Haman must have felt. Haman had just dressed Mordecai in royal robes, paraded him through the streets of Susa on a royal steed, and proclaimed to all, "Thus shall it be done to the man whom the king delights to honor."

The worst part of all this? Haman himself had suggested such pageantry to the king without realizing that the king intended to bestow it on another person. Frankly, ego and opportunity should happen decades apart.

Humility and a humble heart are exalted throughout Scripture, as we saw in Day 1. As the director yells, "Action!" on today's lesson, those traits once again move to center stage.

Read Esther 6:12–14.

After Haman escorts Mordecai through the streets proclaiming Mordecai's greatness, what does Mordecai do?

Mordecai went back to business as usual. The pomp and circumstance did not deter Mordecai from returning to quietly and efficiently serve the king. Ovations do not change humble hearts, because their service does not hinge on applause.

What does Colossians 3:23–25 say?

Mordecai was serving at the gate where the Lord placed him while keeping a protective watch over Esther. His humble response honored God because his value was not dictated by crowd approval. He did not take selfies of himself in royal regalia. God seeks to honor the humble because the humble seek to honor God.

Haman's reaction, however, was polar opposite. In Esther 6:12, how did Haman return home?

Haman felt completely humiliated and rushed home with his head covered as though he was grieving for the dead. That irony is so thick you can cut it with a sword. Haman was so obsessed over destroying Mordecai and the Jews that he never heard God's warning sirens. It is pointless to warn someone of pending danger if the person refuses to hear.

Watching Haman's actions perfectly describes what Jesus taught as He reclined in the home of a prominent Pharisee. What did Jesus say in Luke 14:11?

Haman is humiliated and runs home to coddle his wounded ego. However, he finds little solace there. Once his wife and friends hear what happened, what do they tell Haman in Esther 6:13?

This is yet another moment when I wish cameras had been invented. These were the same people who told Haman to build the gallows in the first place! People who offer bad advice seldom accept responsibility when situations turn sour. But Haman's day is not over yet.

Read Esther 6:14.

What is the first word?

While. While is a time word. It denotes present movement. We see it in phrases such as "She was talking on the phone while she was walking into the library." *While* Haman complained to his wife about having to laud Mordecai in the streets, *while* he covered his head and mourned over everything that had happened that day, *while* his mind was still reeling, the king's eunuchs appeared to escort Haman to Esther's second banquet.

God used Haman's *while* to ensure that Haman did not have time to formulate a getaway plan. *While* Haman fretted, God fenced him in so that nothing prevented His perfect rescue plan for the Jews.

God often accomplishes much in the time increment of *while*. In fact, it describes how He asks us to live and serve Him. *While* God is moving around the pieces in our lives, *while* God is teaching us through formal education or experience, *while* God is loving us in spite of our impatience, He asks that we continue to serve Him with gladness.

The most powerful *while* in all of Scripture occurs in Romans 5:8. Write it here:

While we were still sinners. No matter what you did yesterday, what you are doing today, or what you plan to do tomorrow, *while* you still sin, Jesus still died for you.

So the curtain falls on today's lesson with a picture of Haman's back as the king's eunuchs escort him to Esther's second banquet.

DAY 4
Evil Unmasked

Then Queen Esther answered, "If I have found favor in
your sight, O king, and if it please the king, let my life be
granted to me for my wish, and my people for my request.
For we have been sold, I and my people, to be destroyed, to
be killed, and to be annihilated. If we had been sold merely
as slaves, men and women, I would have been silent, for
our affliction is not be compared with the loss to the king."
Then King Ahasuerus said to Queen Esther, "Who is he,
and where is he, who has dared to do this?" And Esther
said, "A foe and enemy! This wicked Haman!" Then Haman was terrified before the king and the queen.

(Esther 7:3–6)

Once again, the table is lavishly set as Esther prepares to welcome the
king and Haman for the second banquet. Every verse in the Book of Esther
has led up to this pivotal moment.

Haman had just returned home in humiliation after being forced to parade Mordecai through the streets as the conquering hero. He began to realize that perhaps trouble was afoot. He had foolishly organized the genocide
of an entire race of people, a member of whom the king had just delighted
to honor.

Read Esther 7:1–6.

The fragrance of a delicious banquet still clings to the curtains as the
king reclines to enjoy his wine and stimulating conversation. He has not
forgotten that an unanswered question still hangs in the air from Esther's
first banquet. He turns his attention to Esther once again.

In Esther 7:2, what does the king ask Esther?

For the second time, Ahasuerus respectfully addresses his wife as Queen Esther. Kings were accustomed to people asking for favors or material possessions. He knew how to play the courtier game of give-and-take very well. Very little surprised him . . . until tonight.

For the second time, what does he offer Esther?

As we learned earlier in this study, the king was not literally offering Esther half of the kingdom. It was simply how he conveyed that he was open to graciously answering a request.

The author now records the fifth time Esther speaks. What does she tell the king in Esther 7:3–4?

Not once did Esther ask anything for herself. Aside from the fact that she was a Jew and would be saved along with her people, she never made a request to the king solely for self-beneficial reasons. Her requests were centered on the good of *all* her people.

How often do your requests to God center on the needs of others?

Esther wisely realized that she needed to keep her request personal. As Ahasuerus reclined, full of wine and gazing at his beautiful wife, hearing that someone was threatening her life was infinitely more persuasive than a faceless people group. Esther does not identify herself by her heritage, but by her fate: *"Let my life be granted to me. . . . For we have been sold, I and my people."*

When tense situations escalate, it is important to be as clear as possible. The king's confusion is almost palpable. "Wait, isn't Esther a Persian? *What?*" Ahasuerus's unspoken affection for Esther is seen here when he chooses not to berate her from keeping such a huge secret from him.

When Esther finally tells the king her request, she makes it clear that she would have been silent had she been sold into slavery. Wisely, she was conveying that being the king's slave was an honor. But they were planning to kill her, not enslave her.

After hearing such a shocking request, how does the king respond in Esther 7:5?

You can almost sense the king's mounting rage as he asks two questions:

1. Who is he?

   Who is it that plans to kill my wife and her people? The king demands to know the face of his wife's enemy, because that face is now his enemy. This is the point in the drama where a woman's romantic heart throbs over being protected.

2. Where is he?

   Not only *who* is he but *where* is he? Ahasuerus wants the name and the location to confront his wife's deadly foe. Well, guess who's coming to dinner?

In Esther 7:6, how does she respond?

Talk about a dramatic moment in this cinematic masterpiece! This is the point where the orchestra's symbols finally crash loud after a prolonged tympani roll of doom. The camera zooms in for a dramatic close-up of Haman's terror-filled face. Finally! Evil is unmasked and laid bare for all to witness!

Even though we may feel a sense of vindication, God takes no pleasure in condemning the wicked. How do you see God's grief in these passages?

Ezekiel 33:11

2 Peter 3:9

Matthew 23:37

Luke 15:7, 10

As much as we may secretly celebrate Haman's impending downfall, we acknowledge God's grief over such loss. Write out whom God desires to be saved according to the following verses:

Ezekiel 18:23

1 Timothy 2:4

Both Old and New Testaments confirm that our loving God desires for all people to turn from sin and be saved. The life of His Son was proof of that desire.

As Haman is unmasked, Ahasuerus's sleepless night becomes significant. The king learned that Mordecai had never been honored for saving his life. If Mordecai had been honored earlier, at the time the royal assassination plot was uncovered, this critical moment would never have happened.

The text is silent about why the king waited so long, but the providence of God's perfect timing shines bright here. God is in charge of the universe, people, and schedules. And at the perfect time, God reminds Ahasuerus that he had a true, sacrificial servant in Mordecai.

God's perfect timing echoes through the pages of Scripture. For instance, God kept Joseph in prison until the right time to rise to power (Genesis 40:23–41:1). God selected the precise day to free His people from Egyptian slavery (Exodus 12:40–42). And most important, God chose the precise moment for Jesus to be born in Bethlehem *"when the fullness of time had come"* (Galatians 4:4, emphasis added).

God's postponements are not God's procrastinations. We often struggle with impatience, but His patience has a specific purpose: to bring the wicked to repentance. Yes, even egotistical, self-centered Haman and all those like him throughout the ages.

What if Esther had taken credit for revealing the royal assassination plot? Had Esther not rightly given proper credit to Mordecai for saving the king's life, this story would have ended vastly differently.

We close today's lesson on a cliff-hanger of an unmasked villain waiting his fate. Take time here to pause and notice God's perfect timing in your life. Write them in the margin as a reminder that His love is always moving in your life. Keep pressing on, sister!

DAY 5
Victory over the Enemy

And the king arose in his wrath from the wine-drinking
and went into the palace garden, but Haman stayed to
beg for his life from Queen Esther, for he saw that harm
was determined against him by the king. And the king
returned from the palace garden to the place where they
were drinking wine, as Haman was falling on the couch
where Esther was. And the king said, "Will he even assault
the queen in my presence, in my own house?" As the word
left the mouth of the king, they covered Haman's face. . . .
So they hanged Haman on the gallows that he had prepared for Mordecai. Then the wrath of the king abated.

(Esther 7:7–8, 10)

One of the things that scares the living daylights out of me is when
someone unexpectedly startles me. I am the last person at whom you want
to jump out from behind a bush and yell, *"Surprise!"* You may experience
my handbag upside your head or burst eardrums from my bloodcurdling
screams. Most people react poorly to being startled, and King Ahasuerus
was no different.

We left off in yesterday's lesson where Esther landed the proverbial gut
punch to Haman by identifying him as the wicked foe and enemy. As Ahasuerus learns that Haman has arranged the death of his wife and all of her
people, an unmasked, terrified Haman faces a *very* angry king. Cue the
orchestra's "doom" music in the background as we continue the story.

Read Esther 7:7–10.

After Esther unmasks Haman as the true villain, a furious Ahasuerus
storms out. In a commendable moment of self-awareness, the king realizes
that a knee-jerk retaliatory action may not be the best. First, he must get his
emotions under control.

Many a king has made terrible decisions in fits of anger. Remember Nebuchadnezzar? Perhaps Ahasuerus also realized that he could not properly

make a critical decision about Haman's fate through a haze of betrayal and anger.

As Ahasuerus storms out, from whom does Haman beg for his life in verse 7?

Haman's actions clearly reveal that he knew that the real power *did not* lie with the most powerful man in the empire, but with the most powerful *woman.* Esther firmly held Haman's fate in her hands. After all, who would the king condemn? His devoted, beautiful wife or the one who put her in harm's way?

As she unveiled the villain, Esther deployed every clever skill she possessed to avoid implicating the king in any wrongdoing. Imagine the king's shock when he realized that by *his decree* he had unwittingly consented to his wife's execution. By Esther's avoiding accusatory language, perhaps the king's guilt would be redirected toward her enemy. The full force of Esther's words was designed to land on Haman alone.

On a personal level, perhaps Ahasuerus also grappled with two harder issues. His wife had concealed her nationality and his favored prime minister had leveraged his privileged position for a personal vendetta.

Have you ever had to absorb betrayal and eventually forgive? If so, what happened?

Forgiving someone who has intentionally betrayed you is one of the hardest things God asks us to do on planet Earth. Forgive each other, and then love each other. Depending on the person, both can feel impossible at times. But *nothing* is impossible with God (Luke 1:37).

In Esther 7:8 when the king finally cools off and returns, where does he find Haman?

According to Herodotus, it was an ancient Near East custom to recline on couches while eating. (We also see this custom in Amos 6:4–7.) However, for a man to be found on the same couch as any member of the king's harem—much less the queen herself—was met with immediate dire consequences.

Haman had fallen on Esther's couch out of fear, but it was a grave breach of Persian protocol. Haman realized that any power or influence he possesses came only from the king's favor. Such favor had just evaporated in a heartbeat. Haman grabbed Esther's feet and kissed them repeatedly while pleading for his life. The Agagite bully was reduced to a cowering beggar.

Again, the author uses irony. Haman, who demanded Mordecai the Jew to bow before him, now finds himself at the feet of Esther the Jew.

As the king's eyes take in the unbelievable scene in Esther 7:8, what does he ask?

The king's rage and indignation reverberate on the page. After learning that he has been betrayed, Ahasuerus returns to find Haman on his wife's couch. He immediately assumes the worst. What a sight for the king to find just as he was trying to calm down! Rage is invariably a huge stumbling block, especially for kings.

What does Proverbs 16:14 say about a king's rage?

In Proverbs 19:12, to what is a king's rage compared?

The king's guards needed no further instruction. At the end of Esther 7:8, what did they do as soon as the king finished his outraged question?

That is another significant timing reference. *"As the word left the mouth of the king ..."* The Hebrew meaning for that phrase *(haddabar)* references a legal judgment. In other words, as those words left the king's mouth, he effectively ordered Haman's execution.

Reread Esther 7:9–10.

Verse 7:9 begins with another time word: *then.* First, we had *while;* now we have *then.* Then, the eunuchs became tattletales. They tell Ahasuerus about the gallows that Haman had built for Mordecai. The fact that they ratted Haman out points to his unpopularity. You don't tattle on friends.

Here, the author includes yet another momentous irony and reversal of fortune. The very gallows that were built for Mordecai's execution would instead accommodate its creator's capital punishment. Chiastic contrasts fill the pages of Scripture.

Write out Proverbs 11:6.

How does this verse apply to Haman's situation?

This proverb teaches through contrasts, a technique embraced by Esther's author. For example, the people were confused, while Haman celebrated (Esther 3:15); Haman anticipated honor only to be forced to bestow it on Mordecai (Esther 6:11–12); and Haman's plot to kill Mordecai resulted in his own death.

Consequently, without fanfare, a trial, or further conversation, Ahasuerus executed his prime minister. None of Haman's power, wealth, or self-appointed glory could save him in the end. The wrath of the king was abated only after blood was shed and sin mitigated.

The word *abated* in Esther 7:10 ("pacified" in the KJV) is translated in Hebrew to describe the retreating waters of the flood in Genesis 8:1. Our heavenly King's flooding wrath over our sin has been abated by Jesus' blood shed on the cross. In God's perfect timing, Jesus became human to bring about our salvation for such a time as this.

What does 1 Peter 1:18–19 tell us about the cost of our redemption?

Esther 7:7–10 reveals the character of this drama's main players. Prideful Haman had a cowardly heart. Weak Ahasuerus was easily influenced. And courageous Esther was resolute.

One thing is crystal clear: whenever we allow worldly power or position to define us, the Lord will cause a reversal of fortunes that bring us to a crossroads of repentance or destruction.

Even though the villain has been defeated, God's chosen people are still approaching genocide. What can be done to alter an irrevocable death decree? Come back tomorrow, sister.

LESSON 7

Grace Decreed

Esther 8

The irrevocable decree of death against the Jews and the counter decree of life are both given from the same authority—the king's signet ring. Just as King Ahasuerus could not merely withdraw the first decree of death, God cannot merely withdraw the decree of death pronounced against mankind in the Garden of Eden. In its place, God issued a counter decree of life—the Gospel of Jesus Christ. Both are given by the same authority—the King of kings! When we pass from this dark world into God's eternal light, that is the greatest reversal of all time.

- **DAY 1**   Faithful Reward *(Esther 8:1–2)*
- **DAY 2**   Approaching the King . . . Again *(Esther 8:3–6)*
- **DAY 3**   Standing Together *(Esther 8:7–8)*
- **DAY 4**   Grace over Genocide *(Esther 8:9–14)*
- **DAY 5**   Light Triumphs over Darkness *(Esther 8:15–17)*

KEY QUESTIONS

- Do you honor God with the way you react to the challenges in your life?
- Looking back on your life so far, when did God work silently behind the scenes for your benefit? What happened?
- How has that hindsight knowledge affected your spiritual journey?

DAY 1
Faithful Reward

On that day King Ahasuerus gave to Queen Esther the
house of Haman, the enemy of the Jews. And Mordecai
came before the king, for Esther had told what he was to
her.

(Esther 8:1)

In those times there was darkness everywhere. In heaven and on earth,
all the gates of compassion seemed to have been closed.

The killer killed and the Jews died and the outside world adopted an
attitude either of complicity or of indifference.

Only a few had the courage to care.

Elie Wiesel[20]

Elie Wiesel was fifteen years old when the Nazis arrived in his close-knit Jewish community of Sighet, Romania, in March of 1944. The Nazis deported his entire village in sealed cattle cars to concentration camps in Poland. When they arrived at Auschwitz, Elie was separated from his mother and sister and never saw them again. He and his father were able to stay together for nearly a year, until his father finally succumbed to starvation and exhaustion. On April 11, 1945, Elie and the remaining victims of the Buchenwald concentration camp were mercifully liberated by American troops.

Several years ago, after I read his critically acclaimed book *Night,* I could not properly digest food for over a week. *Night* recounted his experiences as a Jewish prisoner in the Auschwitz and Buchenwald concentration camps during World War II. The horrors that he and his fellow prisoners suffered shook me to the core. His blunt account provided a hellish insight into dark places, where God did not reign in human hearts.

Those thirteen months changed Elie and the entire trajectory of his life. He eventually moved to America, where he became the voice for victims of genocide and suffering around the world as a human rights activist and prolific author. In 1985, he was awarded the Congressional Gold Medal, followed by the Nobel Peace Prize in 1986. I wish I could have met him before he died in 2016. He was living proof of how God can bring good out of absolutely every situation, if we let Him. Elie Wiesel demonstrated the difference that one person can make against the tide of genocide.

As chapter 8 opens in Esther, we behold the tide of genocide slowly beginning to turn. Ahasuerus has executed Haman, the plot's mastermind. Rays of hope begin to illuminate the gloom of a seemingly impossible situation. *NIV* *New Int'l Vers* *King Xerxes?*

Read Esther 8:1–2.

These verses begin by revealing a quick succession of reversals of fortune. In verse 1, what did Esther receive? *the Estate of Haman, the enemy of the Jews. And Mordecai Came I the presence of, King for Esther had w f. King 8:E w related Verse 2 King y signate ring relained Haman + presented Mordecia, Ester Ester appointed him over*

We will call this a *Fiscal Reversal*. As a former orphan adopted by her cousin, Esther had likely not owned such riches in her entire life. It reminds me of lottery winners who become millionaires in an instant. Reminiscent of a Robin Hood deed, all of the wealth and possessions that Haman owned now belonged to Esther. *The wealth of the ungodly will eventually find its way into the hands of the*

What does Proverbs 13:22 say about a sinner's wealth? *righteous for whom it has been laid up for.*

Haman presumably spent his whole life building his riches and his own kingdom, and for what? He would not live to enjoy his comfort in retirement. In fact, he did not even live long enough to find out that his sons would not inherit his life's accumulations either. He built on a shaky foundation of human cunning and human efforts.

What have you spent the majority of your life building? *love, mercy, Compassion*

Jesus states that those who hear His words & do them are wise builders. They have built

According to Matthew 7:24-27, on what foundation does our life need to be built to withstand life's storm? *their homes on rock solid foundations. The winds howl, the rains come — even a flood comes — but the house stands firm. Those who hear His words buts. fail to live by them are foolish builders.*

Those verses represent the last words that Jesus preached in the Sermon on the Mount. He taught invaluable truths in that sermon, yet these words from Matthew 7:24-27 were the last. When you hear a sermon, which words are usually the ones you remember most? The wrap-up. The final thoughts that tie the whole story together.

And the main storyline of the Sermon on the Mount is salvation. Salvation happens instantaneously; however, strengthening your spiritual foundation—your life—through the Word of God is a continuing process.

The king handed over all of Haman's worldly possessions to Esther. In fact, Esther 8:1 says that it happened *"on that day."* Haman's body was not even cold when Esther received his fortunes. Since Ahasuerus loved to acquire wealth to finance military ambitions, this action may reveal hidden guilt rather than generosity. The king had blindly trusted Haman, which resulted in the difficulties that Esther and her people were now facing.

At the end of Esther 8:1, what did Esther reveal to the king? *Who she was*

This is the first time that the king and Mordecai actually meet face-to-face. Imagine the king's surprise at learning that Mordecai is Esther's cousin! The man who saved the king's life is now related to him through marriage. Consequently, what does the king do in Esther 8:2? *took off his signate ring that he reclaimed from Haman & gave to mordecia*

205

Let's call this a *Career Reversal.* We learned in Esther 3:10 that the king's signet ring was a sign of authority to seal official documents on the king's behalf. The king had someone run to Haman's corpse to retrieve the ring so that he could give it to Mordecai.

Mordecai was now the Persian prime minister, living in his predecessor's house and wearing that authoritative bling. Is it any wonder that Ahasuerus trusted both Mordecai and Esther? Mordecai saved his life, and Esther served him faithfully. God put the right cousins in the right place at the right time.

Despite difficult circumstances, God is faithful to Esther and Mordecai. Pause for a moment to ponder how God has been faithful in your life when your days seemed darkest. What happened? *blesses me with ways to help other.*

What about this past week? When has God proven faithful within the past seven days? *Financially to help Jay*

Rom 8:28

Those who love God and are called according to His purpose never need to worry about jeopardizing God's unwavering faithfulness. Such a strong foundation inspires us to look to Christ's faithfulness, which stirs our courage, bravery, and faith.

As we leave today's lesson, the drama is ramping up once again. Even though God has blessed Esther and Mordecai with favor and success, the king's first decree to annihilate the Jews still sits in the middle of Ahasuerus' elaborate courtyard like the proverbial pink elephant. We leave today's lesson with inspiration from the words of Elie Wiesel as he accepted the Nobel Peace Prize:

I remember: it happened yesterday or eternities ago. A young

Jewish boy discovered the kingdom of night. I remember his bewilderment; I remember his anguish. It all happened so fast. The ghetto. The deportation. The sealed cattle car. The fiery altar upon which the history of our people and the future of mankind were meant to be sacrificed.

I remember: he asked his father: "Can this be true? This is the twentieth century, not the Middle Ages. Who would allow such crimes to be committed? How could the world remain silent?"

And now the boy is turning to me: "Tell me," he asks.

"What have you done with my future? What have you done with your life?"

And I tell him that I have tried. That I have tried to keep memory alive, that I have tried to fight those who would forget.

Because if we forget, we are guilty, we are accomplices.[21]

(Oslo, Norway; December 10, 1986)

DAY 2
Approaching the King . . . Again

Then Esther spoke again to the king. She fell at his feet and
wept and pleaded with him to avert the evil plan of Haman
the Agagite and the plot that he had devised against the
Jews. When the king held out the golden scepter to Esther,
Esther rose and stood before the king. And she said, "If it
please the king, and if I have found favor in his sight, and
if the thing seems right before the king, and I am pleasing
in his eyes, let an order be written to revoke the letters
devised by Haman the Agagite, the son of Hammedatha,
which he wrote to destroy the Jews who are in all the provinces of the king. For how can I bear to see the calamity
that is coming to my people? Or how can I bear to see the
destruction of my kindred?"

(Esther 8:3–6)

When a hero and heroine conquer the evil villain and receive their reward, the story usually reads *The End*. At this point, however, Esther and
Mordecai's story remains anticlimactic. As we learned in Lesson 1, Day 5,
the laws of the Medes and Persians cannot be revoked or changed. Consequently, Haman's first decree is still in effect. The Jews still face genocide.
There is still much work to do as Esther trusts God and plunges ahead.

Read Esther 8:3–6.

There is a significant difference in Esther 8:3 and Esther 4:15–16. The
first time Esther approached the king, she balked and had to be prompted
by Mordecai's passionate plea. In fact, the first time Esther approached the
king to request his presence at dinner in Esther 4, the Apocrypha adds:

She was radiant with perfect beauty, and she looked happy, as if
beloved, but her heart was frozen with fear. When she had gone
through all the doors, she stood before the king. He was seat-
ed on his royal throne, clothed in the full array of his majesty,
all covered with gold and precious stones. And he was most

terrifying. Lifting his face, flushed with splendor, he looked at her in fierce anger. And the queen faltered and turned pale and faint and collapsed upon the head of the maid who went before her.

(Addition D, 15:5–7)[22]

Esther is portrayed in the Apocrypha as fearful and fainting. Esther 4 records that Esther was fearful, but resolute. Either way, Esther was afraid. Here in Esther 8:3, she approaches the king without hesitation.

What do Esther's actions reveal? *She feels*

Esther has now stepped into the leadership position that God planned for her all along. She does not even consult Mordecai on what course of action to take or words to speak before she approaches Ahasuerus. Esther's actions also reveal that she feels more secure in her relationship with her husband. The king had protected Esther and her people when Haman's evil was unmasked. Security and feeling safe rank high on a woman's list of basic needs. By fighting *for* her and not *against* her, the king helped Esther feel more secure about approaching him a second time.

However, she is still careful to follow court etiquette. What does Esther do in Esther 8:3?

She shows Ahasuerus the respect to which he is entitled. But here again, Esther's actions are different than the first time she approached the king.

What is Esther's request in 5:4? *To come to the banquet*

And what is her request in Esther 8:5?

reverse the decree to destroy the Jews

Did you notice the drastic difference in Esther's demeanor? The first time, she was cool, proper, and gracious. Not this time. The clock against her people ticks in the background, so she gets straight to the point in a dramatic scene. We have seen Esther stand to face the king, sit and dine with the king, yet now she falls and weeps at his feet. Desperation always suspends pretense and reveals honesty. She had been strong for so long, but time for her people was growing short.

Have you ever been strong for yourself and others over an extended period when hard circumstances happened? If so, when? *Prison*

Did you grow fatigued or weary over time? If so, what happened?

pray

No matter how long we stand strong, we all have a breaking point. Esther had been swept into the palace, into the king's bedchamber, and into Persian court life. Then she discovered both her and her people had been selected for elimination. Mordecai not-so-gently reminded her that the hope of an entire people rested on her shoulders. Then she invited her enemy to dinner, betrayed his evil intentions to the king, and watched as he was carted away to the gallows.

Is it any wonder that Esther finally falls down weeping? If pressure-packed times ever broke you, at whose feet did you fall?

the lord

Write out the reassuring words from Psalm 23:6.

Surely goodness + mercy shall follow me all the days of my life + I shall dwell in the house of the Lord forever

The Lord provides the reassurance and strength we need every single time we're struggling in battle. We are never abandoned to fall to pieces apart from the Prince of Peace.

Esther falls before the king's feet and proceeds to weep and plea for mercy. Laws passed by the Medes and Persians were irrevocable. Consequently, Esther begs Ahasuerus to issue a second edict that, in effect, countermands his first one. Apparently, Esther was not concerned about who occupied the king's throne room as she pleaded. Let them all hear! Her greater concern was her people, not proper court decorum.

Although we have seen Esther's concern and compassion for her people before now, do you believe when difficulties surface such sentiment that we move more quickly? How?

yes

What cause or group of people bring such care and compassion into your heart? Why? *civil liberties unions*

Yet another irony in the Book of Esther is that while Vashti was deposed for refusing to appear before the king, Esther was raised up for appearing uninvited.

We leave this lesson as Esther stands in front of Ahasuerus to ask for the life of her and her people. She does not ask without hope. We cannot miss the important point of today's lesson: *Esther's intercession in the throne room before the king was the catalyst that saved her people from genocide.* When you and I enter the throne room of God in intercessory prayer, God moves mountains.

As Esther's bravery increases, God begins to swing the tide of favor toward His people. We see once again how no attempt to destroy God's children can succeed. God's covenant love for Israel will be—and is being—fulfilled.

DAY 3
Standing Together

Then King Ahasuerus said to Queen Esther and to Mordecai the Jew, "Behold, I have given Esther the house of Haman, and they have hanged him on the gallows, because he intended to lay hands on the Jews. But you may write as you please with regard to the Jews, in the name of the king, and seal it with the king's ring, for an edict written in the name of the king and sealed with the king's signet ring cannot be revoked."

(Esther 8:7–8)

In the spring of 1995, I arrived one morning at the law firm, where I settled into my routine of legal secretarial tasks. When the partner for whom I worked arrived, he announced that he was leaving the firm, taking several attorneys with him, and he wanted me to join them.

I had been his secretary for only six months, so it would be a leap of faith. I was only in my late twenties, so it was a huge honor to be asked to serve as an office managing partner's assistant. I also realized that I was significantly *underpaid* for this new demanding position and increased responsibilities.

That night, I prayed for God to give me the strength and appropriate words to ask for my first ever salary increase. I was struggling financially, so my prayer included lots of tears and begging. The worst outcome would be for him to say no, and I would stay where I was—unless the current firm no longer needed me after he left. Such a request would put my livelihood on the line.

The next morning, as soon as the partner settled into his office, I calmly stated my case to him with hands shaking so hard that I had to clench them together in my lap. He asked for the salary figure that I had in mind. I had done extensive research the night before, so I was ready for his question. He promised to make a few calls and would let me know after lunch.

Needless to say, I could not swallow a single bite of my lunch that day, so instead I prayed. The new firm came back with a phenomenal salary increase and benefits package offer, which I joyfully accepted. I had prayed for crumbs, but God provided the whole cake, plus frosting. When I arrived home after work that day, I burst into tears and thanked God for his over-abundant provision and goodness.

Esther's drama picks up today in mid-scene as she stands before the king, the evidence of fresh tears still on her cheeks. She has requested Ahasuerus to spare the life of her people and rescue them from Haman's genocidal decree. Can you imagine the lightning fast prayer for her people that likely flashed through Esther's mind? This is the moment she's been working toward. She states her case and holds her breath to hear the king's verdict.

Read Esther 8:7–8.

The king starts off by reminding Esther of his generosity to her and Mordecai regarding Haman's property. He also reminds her of his eventual benevolence toward the Jews. I guess we cannot expect a king to be modest.

In verse 8, what does the king give Esther permission to do?

Write another decree in the kings name behalf of the Jews + seal it with the signet ring - no document can be revoked

Even though Ahasuerus does not mention Mordecai, his involvement is assumed since he now possesses the king's signet ring. The king gives Esther free reign to confer with her cousin and write a decree that counteracts the first one.

It comes as no surprise that the king is uninterested in details. The first time he handed over his signet ring, he allowed Haman a free hand to decree genocide. The second time he hands over his signet ring, he allows Esther and Mordecai a free hand to reverse the tide. It appears that Ahasuerus has no problem giving someone else the power to issue edicts bearing his seal. Self-absorption allows little room for empathy or meaningful growth.

Self-absorbed leaders have caused much damage over the course of history. Nero, Herod, and Nebuchadnezzar come to mind, to name just a few. Unfortunately, God's people were always their targets. However, there are also several instances in Scripture where great men of faith enter God's throne room to pray on Israel's behalf.

Who is praying in the following verses for Israel and why?

Exodus 32:7–14

[handwritten: Moses prayed after people of Egypt remember your servants Abraham Isaac Israel that you said I will noble you descents as numerous as the stars (who made a golden calf + the Lord relented his threat.]

Nehemiah 1:4–11

[handwritten: pray Israelites pray remember what you said to Moses - I will scatter you but if you return home, I will grant favor]

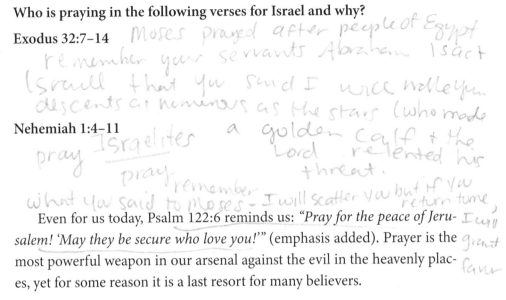

Even for us today, Psalm 122:6 reminds us: *"Pray for the peace of Jerusalem! 'May they be secure who love you!'"* (emphasis added). Prayer is the most powerful weapon in our arsenal against the evil in the heavenly places, yet for some reason it is a last resort for many believers.

Yale scholar and evangelist R. A. Torrey once wrote:

> The Devil is perfectly willing that the church should multiply its organizations and its deftly-contrived machinery for the conquest of the world for Christ, if it will only give up praying.[23]

One passionate believer devoted to prayer can make a powerful difference, because prayer unleashes the power of God. Esther had fasted (which is usually accompanied by prayer) along with Mordecai and all the Israelites for the strength to face and overcome Haman's evil edict. *Prayer is vital.*

The evil work of Haman placed in jeopardy all of God's covenant promises to Israel. So God raised up Esther for such a time as this to lead the dramatic rescue with His covenant love leading the charge. Esther had prayed for crumbs of freedom, but God provided the whole cake, plus frosting.

DAY 4
Grace over Genocide

And he wrote in the name of King Ahasuerus and sealed
it with the king's signet ring. Then he sent the letters by
mounted couriers riding on swift horses . . . saying that the
king allowed the Jews who were in every city to gather and
defend their lives, to destroy, to kill, and to annihilate any
armed force of any people or province that might attack
them.

(Esther 8:10–11)

When the king granted Esther the power to draft and distribute a new
decree, she did not let the grass grow under her dainty feet. Esther, Mordecai, and the Persian Jews had prayed for this moment; by God's grace, it
had finally arrived.

Read Esther 8:9–14.

What happened first according to the first sentence in verse 9?

**Esther and Mordecai wasted no time getting to work, because time was
not on their side. They immediately summoned the royal scribes and
began dictating the language of the new decree. According to the second
sentence of verse 9, who was drafting the decree?**

It makes sense for Mordecai to undertake that task. After all, he was a
government official who spent countless hours at the king's gate. He knew
exactly what needed to be written and how to write it. He also knew the
procedure for royal decrees, because he followed almost the identical pro-

cedure that Haman had when the original decree was sent out.

In verse 9, to whom is the new decree sent?

In Esther 3:12, to whom was Haman's original decree sent?

Mordecai understood the process, which certainly makes the whole process more manageable. Preparation is key. Being present is also key. In other words, Mordecai had likely spent years preparing for and serving in his official Persian capacity; however, Mordecai also had to be present among others to retain connections and keep up to date on the latest so that he knew where and how to send the new decree to all Persians.

Mordecai and Esther's counter decree granted three key components for the Jews:

1. They could defend their lives.

2. They could take the life of the one attacking them.

3. They could plunder the goods of their attackers.

Mordecai would likely not have known to include all those elements aside from careful planning and diligent inquiries. Their main concern was staying alive; however, Mordecai broadened the scope.

1. Defend Their Lives

The primary function of the decree was to preserve the lives of the Jews, including Esther and Mordecai. All life is precious to God, yet it was especially crucial to save His chosen people according to His covenant promise, since through them one day would come the Messiah.

2. Kill Their Attackers

The decree went even further to grant the Jews permission to attack those who attacked them. They were no longer required to simply stand there and face death without using every defense possible to attack back—perhaps to drive the attackers away faster or to change the mind of the attackers altogether.

3. Plunder Their Attackers' Goods

Finally, the decree allowed the Jews to plunder their attackers' goods. That was basically the financial version of an eye for an eye.

Mordecai thought of the Jewish people's core needs as he set out to do what the Lord had positioned him to accomplish. This begs the question: Have you determined what you need to ask from your heavenly King during this season of your life?

If so, in what position has He placed you to accomplish it?

If it is not clear, spend some time in prayer right now and ask God to reveal it to you.

In what way has God placed you in such a time as this to accomplish something—no matter how great or small?

Mordecai did not undertake the task alone. He collaborated with Esther and deployed the king's messengers to spread the word. The Jews' ticking death bomb would have gone off if Mordecai had been left to do all of the cleanup work alone. He would have simply run out of time.

Sometimes when we have needs, we hesitate to ask the right people for help. Whether out of fear or something else, have you ever chosen not to ask for help from someone you knew, even though you knew they could provide it? Why or why not?

In the most significant reversal of fortunes, Mordecai issues a decree that counters Haman's decree. From Esther 3:13, fill in the language from the first decree:

> "Letters were sent by couriers to all the king's provinces with instruction to _____, to _____, and to _____ all Jews."

Now from Esther 8:10–11, fill in the language from the second decree:

> "Then he sent the letters by mounted couriers . . . saying that the king allowed the Jews who were in every city to gather and defend their lives, to _____, to _____, and to _____ any armed force of any people or province that might attack them."

Let's call this a *Legal Reversal*. Haman drafted an irrevocable law, sealed with the king's signet ring, ordering all Persian Jews annihilated. Since a law of the Medes and Persians could not be revoked, Ahasuerus now grants Mordecai and Esther the authority to countermand Haman's original decree by allowing the Jews to defend themselves.

The second decree was worded in such a way as to neutralize royal retribution so that Jews could defend themselves without their actions being construed as rebellion against the crown. Basically, it put the Jews and enemies on a level playing field. The Apocrypha includes the wording of this second degree. In relevant parts, it says:

> For Haman son of Hamadathos, a Macedonian, . . . unable to restrain his arrogance, he undertook to deprive us of our kingdom and our life and with intricate craft and deceit asked for the destruction of Mordecai, our savior and perpetual benefactor, and of Esther, the blameless partner of our kingdom, together with their whole nation. . . . Therefore post a copy of this letter publicly in every place and permit the Jews to live under their own laws. And give them reinforcements, so that on the thirteenth day of the twelfth month, Adar, on that very day they may defend themselves against those who attack them at the time of their affliction. For God, who rules over all things, has made this day to be a joy to his chosen people instead of a day of destruction for them.

(Addition E, 16:10, 12–13, 19–21)[24]

Let's make this practical. Imagine that you are serving in the Persian military. You love the first decree because it means you get to kill without retribution and plunder the goods of every Judean you kill. But now the second decree gives Jews the authority to defend themselves, including killing you and plundering your goods. With Decree 2 in place, you would probably reconsider acting on Decree 1, because if you act on Decree 1, you are now under the consequences of Decree 2. That alone likely caused several would-be Persian attackers to sheath their swords.

Have you ever been in such a situation where you had to rethink your actions because changing circumstances made your proposed actions more unfavorable? If so, what was the circumstance? What happened?

As we close today's lesson, we see God's abundant grace as He once again prevents the planned annihilation of the Israelites. The king's first decree was designed to take away life; his second decree offered the chance at life.

God's punishment of sin was designed to take away life. However, His decree of love through Jesus Christ offers us a second chance at eternal life for all who believe that Jesus died, was buried, and rose again to prepare a mansion for us in heaven. What better plunder exists than a mansion for all eternity with Jesus?

We will be resurrected and live on this earth renewed and restored. In essence, just as Mordecai lived in the home and estate formerly owned by Haman, we will live forever in the new earth that formerly "belonged" to Satan and his followers.

DAY 5
Light Triumphs over Darkness

Then Mordecai went out from the presence of the king in royal robes of blue and white, with a great golden crown and a robe of fine linen and purple, and the city of Susa shouted and rejoiced. The Jews had light and gladness and joy and honor. And in every province and in every city, wherever the king's command and his edict reached, there was gladness and joy among the Jews, a feast and a holiday. And many from the peoples of the country declared themselves Jews, for fear of the Jews had fallen on them.

(Esther 8:15–17)

I'll never forget the first time I rushed to the hospital when my older sister went into labor with her first child. I would finally be an auntie, and my excitement was palpable. With flowers and pink balloons in hand, I made it to the hospital in record time.

Now, I am not a woman who desires to witness childbirth. I'm more a north-of-the-sheets kind of auntie, so I waited outside the delivery room. Waiting was so hard! I knew that my sister was in for a long ordeal, but the result would be life. When I finally held my new niece, the tears flowed without ceasing. I was so glad that my sister and niece were perfectly healthy, and I was full of joy to finally hold the gift of life after such a long wait.

That scenario is similar to the state of waiting that the Jews now faced in the Book of Esther. Mordecai and Esther had drafted the decree, sealed it, and distributed it throughout the empire. Even though a long ordeal lay ahead until the day of battle, the result would be life for the Jews amidst much rejoicing.

Read Esther 8:15–17.

How was Mordecai dressed after the decree had been distributed around the empire?

The fine colors and materials used for Mordecai's robes identified him as nobility with a high political position. It was clear that he was a man to whom respect was due. The gold crown did not designate rule, but favor.

Do you remember the first time Mordecai wore royal robes back in chapter 6? When the king discovered that Mordecai saved his life, he ordered (at Haman's unwitting suggestion) that Mordecai be dressed in royal robes and paraded around the city of Susa.

However, those robes were on loan for a specific occasion. Here, the robes now bestowed on Mordecai are his to keep as a sign of his noble status.

When the Jews saw Mordecai, what was their reaction in Esther 8:15?

Here occurs yet another irony. The king had to order people to bow down to Haman, remember? This whole mess started because Mordecai refused to bow to Haman. But the king had to issue no such order here. The people willingly shouted and rejoiced at the sight of Mordecai.

Why do you believe the people respected Mordecai more than Haman?

His relentless, diligent work at the city gate and working with Esther to coordinate this moment had earned the people's respect and loyalty without their being told to extend it. Respect is still valuable in our day. We show elders, military, first responders, teachers, parents, and many others the respect they deserve. Few true, lifelong friendships are formed when respect is absent.

Do you find that true in your close relationships? What is your respect based on?

Respect has little to do with a job or position someone holds; it has everything to do with the person, specifically their character and morals. I can respect the office of President of the United States, but there have certainly been presidents I did not respect personally due to differing values.

Write out Esther 8:16 here:

In Esther 4:3, the Jews were in great mourning over the first law. But after the second law is passed, there is light and gladness. Let's call this an *Emotional Reversal.* After a seemingly endless season of mourning and worry, reprieve has arrived!

What does Nehemiah 8:10 promise?

Our circumstances may appear dark for a while, but joy always comes in the morning. A Christian's joy is not based on fleeting circumstances, but on Jesus Christ alone. Christ makes us new each day, despite how we messed up yesterday or how we will fall short tomorrow.

The joy of the Lord is our strength! The Book of Esther provides abundant encouragement that no matter how dark the night or seemingly absent our God, He is ever-present and ever-watchful.

In Esther 8:17 amidst all of the rejoicing, what did many of the people declare?

The phrase *"declared themselves Jews"* occurs only this once in all of Scripture and has been interpreted in a number of ways. Non-Jews could become Jewish through conversion, by claiming that they were Jews, or simply by associating with Jews. Let's call this a *Spiritual Reversal*. Despite various interpretations, one truth holds for each one: the non-Jews recognized God's mighty hand at work to preserve His chosen people and wanted to be part of it.

God's faithfulness shines through the honor bestowed on Mordecai. As a Benjaminite, an avowed enemy of the Amalekites (Haman's lineage), Mordecai avoided repeating his ancestor King Saul's mistake by being too lenient with God's enemies. There is a reversal of sorts to note here. Because Saul allowed some of the Amalekites to live, he forfeited his crown. Yet because Mordecai chose to stand firm and oppose them, he acquired a crown.

Had Mordecai and Esther not stood firm against God's enemy, the extermination of the Jews would have voided God's messianic promise. And God's rock-solid promises are *never* voided. More than five hundred Old Testament verses reference a coming Messiah. Write out two of them below.

Psalm 2:2

Daniel 9:25–26

Centuries before Jesus walked on the earth, God repeatedly pointed to the future Messiah, whom He would send to sit on the throne of David forever. The Jews functioned as the conduit to fulfill God's promise to the world. Consequently, God worked providentially in the lives of Mordecai and Esther to safeguard His chosen people and preserve that line.

What does God reveal about Israelites in the following verses?

Genesis 12:1–3

Galatians 3:7–9

The Israelites are Abraham's seed and God's chosen people. Through faith, you and I have been grafted into the Vine to bear fruit that lasts for His glory. In Christ, you and I are on the winning side of history, victorious over the troubles of this life.

Nineteenth-century preacher Charles Spurgeon put it like this:

> The foes of the truth of God can never put out the candle which God has lit; they can never crush the living seed which the Lord Jesus has sown in His own blood-bought people.[25]

In an era when neither women nor Jews were valued, God elevated a female Judean exile as an unlikely vessel through whom He would work to save His people. That is a powerful foreshadowing of the salvation God would work through the unlikely vessel of a babe born in Bethlehem.

Reversal of Fortune

Esther 9–10

The day of battle finally arrives. The Jews assemble in their cities on the appointed day to defend themselves from those determined to destroy them. As the battles rage, no one can stand against the Jews—not because their enemies failed to attack, but because God's chosen people cannot be conquered. The Festival of Purim is instituted as the Jews celebrate God's faithfulness in the victory from annihilation from that day and through to today.

- **DAY 1**   On That Very Day *(Esther 9:1)*
- **DAY 2**   Let the Battle Commence *(Esther 9:2–10)*
- **DAY 3**   Justice or Revenge? *(Esther 9:11–16)*
- **DAY 4**   The Feast of Purim *(Esther 9:17–32)*
- **DAY 5**   The Wisdom of Mordecai *(Esther 10:1–3)*

KEY QUESTIONS

- In what event(s) in your life has God turned sorrow into joy?

- Purim includes a day for giving to one another and the poor. What prompts you to give to others?

DAY 1
On That Very Day

Now in the twelfth month, which is the month of Adar, on the thirteenth day of the same, when the king's command and edict were about to be carried out, on the very day when the enemies of the Jews hoped to gain the mastery over them, the reverse occurred: the Jews gained mastery over those who hated them.

(Esther 9:1)

The date is March 7, 473 BC. Dawn reveals an eerie silence despite an overcrowded stage. The day of battle has arrived. Jewish men stand shoulder-to-shoulder, organized, armed, and waiting. Due to Esther's bravery, they have been able to prepare for this moment over many months. As their wives and children huddle offstage in the morning mist, the sound of an advancing Persian army rises in the distance.

On the ancient Hebrew lunar calendar, the thirteenth day of the twelfth month (the month of Adar) fell on March 7, 473 BC. Many dates contained in Esther can be verified with dates recorded in surviving Persian records, which are then easily translated to our modern calendar. It was springtime in Persia. The temperatures were getting warmer, buds of dormant plants were beginning to appear. Yet those pleasures were overshadowed as Persia's Jewish people diligently prepared for war.

The Jews had not asked for nor intentionally invited this trouble. For an American, Pearl Harbor comes to mind. On Sunday, December 7, 1941, at 7:48 a.m., Japanese fighter planes, without provocation, attacked our US military base in Hawaii. The Japanese desired to discourage America's interference in their Pacific pursuits.

However, the attack brought about a complete reversal of their goals. The Japanese attack wakened a sleeping giant who was minding its own business. Within twenty-four hours, the US declared war on Japan, and our involvement in World War II eventually brought about a decisive, resounding defeat of Japan and its allies.

Esther chapter 9 opens with a strikingly similar situation. The Jews had been simply minding their own business when Haman decided to punish Mordecai for bruising his ego. Without provocation, Haman drew up a plan to attack all Jews in the Persian Empire. Little did Haman know that when he put his plan in place, he had provoked a holy giant: the God of Abraham. However, Haman didn't live long enough to see the destruction that his ego-driven temper tantrum eventually caused.

Read Esther 9:1.

Verse 1 uses the word *reverse*. We have looked at many reversals in the Book of Esther. What reversal is described?

The Hebrew word for *reverse* (הפך, *hapak*) used here refers to overturning, changing, or turning back. This same Hebrew word is found in the following verses. What is being changed in each?

1 Samuel 10:9

Exodus 14:5

Lamentations 5:14

Whether changing a heart, a mind, or an object to His will, God is capable of reversing anything to accomplish His purposes.

What is the single biggest reversal that God brought about in your life?

What did it change for you?

How did that change affect your faith walk?

The biggest reversal *by far* that God has brought about in my life is where my soul will spend eternity. Until my early twenties, my eternity was hell, because up to that point I had rejected Jesus as my Lord and Savior. I thought Christianity was for weak, insecure people who couldn't control their life. Well, self-control is the biggest delusion to overcome. When God called me by faith to be enfolded into His forever family, the changes have been nonstop. Some changes I embraced, but some were much harder. Have you found that true in your faith journey, as well?

After an eleven-month wait, the day has finally arrived. The Persian military all across the empire finally move in to attack the Jewish communities. What happened in Esther 9:1?

Those who expected mastery suffered catastrophe. God promises catastrophe for all who seek to suppress and destroy His chosen people.

Write out Jeremiah 30:16 here:

Some may view the Book of Esther as a perseverance tale demonstrating how the Jews stood tall in the midst of struggle to fight for good over evil. Perhaps that is true. However, the larger picture points squarely at the Gospel.

The Book of Esther sends a clear message attesting to every believer's need for complete dependence on God through Jesus Christ, our Mediator, whose sacrifice on Golgotha bridges the gap to offer the hope of eternal deliverance for all.

As the sounds of battle rage around Esther and Mordecai, God's love trumpets victory!

DAY 2
Let the Battle Commence

The Jews gathered in their cities throughout all the provinces of King Ahasuerus to lay hands on those who sought
their harm. And no one could stand against them, for the
fear of them had fallen on all peoples. . . . The Jews struck
all their enemies with the sword, killing and destroying
them, and did as they pleased to those who hated them.

(Esther 9:2, 5)

The Jews meet the enemies head-on amidst clashing swords and battle
cries on the very day they were to celebrate the Passover. Perhaps the Jews
thought they would fight to their death. But God already knew that death
would pass over them—as it did on the very first Passover.

Read Esther 9:2–10.

Write out the second sentence of Esther 9:2.

Do not be lulled into assuming that just because fear had descended
on the enemies that they failed to attack. The phrase "no one could stand
against them" means that no matter how hard the enemies tried, they could
not *conquer* the Jews. There are many instances in Scripture where God
caused fear to fall on the enemies of the Israelites—not a fear of the Jews,
but a fear of their God (Isaiah 2:10; 2 Chronicles 14:13).

**However, God had provided His people with a far more effective weapon
than swords. What does Esther 9:2 say fell on the enemy attackers?**

Not many emotions debilitate us faster than fear. The Hebrew noun for *fear* (פחד, *pachad*) refers to terror or dread. It is the same word used in Exodus 15:16 during the exodus when the Israelites realize that Pharaoh's chariots had trapped them against the Red Sea without escape. Fear appears many times in Job also as he endures severe testing from the Lord.

What causes you to fear?

I do not tend to be a fearful person until I think of something terrible happening to someone I love. As I finish edits on this chapter, the COVID-19 coronavirus pandemic is raging across the globe.

Literally, thousands of news reports have conveyed how families have to say goodbye to their dying loved ones via walkie-talkie, videoconference, or FaceTime because they cannot be together in the same room for fear of spreading the virus. I can think of nothing worse on this earth than watching a loved one die and being unable to hold and comfort them. I am choking up simply writing this.

As Christians, we are instructed to fear the Lord. Not be frightened of the Lord, but to fear Him in reverent awe. Write out the following verses:

1 Samuel 12:24

Acts 9:31

Psalm 128:1

We are to fear the Lord in reverent awe because of the marvelous works He accomplished on our behalf through Jesus Christ's death on the cross. In Him rests the power to raise us from death to life.

Esther 9:3 records that fear of Mordecai also fell on them. That fear is the same word used in Esther 9:2. In verse 3, on whom did the fear of Mordecai fall?

The Persian officials, satraps, governors, and royal agents helped *the Jews* because they feared how powerful Mordecai had become. Let that sink in for a moment. Imagine serving the military arm of the government only to realize that the leaders within your own government are working counterintelligence *against* you because they fear the opposition's leader. War and fear make for strange bunkmates.

As Mordecai's fame and power increased and God's plan moved forward, the Jews successfully defeated every enemy attack. Esther 9:5 provides the climax of this whole drama. Write it out here:

The overarching purpose of the Book of Esther is to tell the story of how God providentially saved His chosen people from genocide. All verses have led us to this very point of triumph as verse 5 narrates the Jews' survival and victory. Apart from the mighty power and loving grace of God, the Jews in this foreign Persian land would have faced certain annihilation that day.

On that "Passover Day," God proved once again that He was still their faithful Deliverer. And for you and me, God's Word in the Old Testament is the truth of deliverance by which we live in light of its New Testament fulfillment in the person of Jesus.

According to Esther 9:6–10, who else did the Jews kill?

I don't know about you, but I find it difficult to read scriptural incidents of mass destruction of life—namely, wars and episodes of seemingly unnecessary carnage. In these verses we see the destruction of all ten of Haman's sons. According to *The Lutheran Study Bible*'s note on 9:7–10, "Killing Haman's sons guaranteed that they would not seek to avenge their father's death or regain his office."

We do not know if the sons followed their father's prejudicial and egotistical characteristics; we know only that in one day, they were all killed. Haman's wife Zeresh is not listed among the slain, so we can only assume that on that day she had to bear the loss of all her children at the same time. Words fail to accurately describe the depth of such pain.

After months of mourning, worry, and dread, March 7, 473 BC, was a day of joy and celebration for Persian Jews. Thanks to Esther's bravery, given to her by God, the Judeans lived to carry out God's promise to deliver a Messiah through them one day.

The Book of Esther opens wide the opportunity for you and me to reflect on the faith that God has given us in this topsy-turvy world. Each day that we live under the protective blood of Jesus Christ, we experience the Passover goodness of His sacrificial love.

DAY 3
Justice or Revenge?

And Esther said, "If it please the king, let the Jews who are
in Susa be allowed tomorrow also to do according to this
day's edict. And let the ten sons of Haman be hanged on
the gallows." So the king commanded this to be done. A
decree was issued in Susa, and the ten sons of Haman were
hanged.

(Esther 9:13–14)

The stage lights come up on a grim battle scene. Property destroyed.
The slain littering the countryside. War is always grim regardless of who
wins. As this portion of the Book of Esther describes the destruction of
thousands of human lives, it can be very unsettling. A natural question to
ask God is "Why did it have to come to that?"

Read Esther 9:11–16.

**As the statistics are given to Ahasuerus in verse 11, how does the king
respond in verse 12?**

As he recounts to Esther the carnage count, which include Haman's
ten sons, we see him wonder out loud what has happened in the rest of his
kingdom. With such a vast empire, apparently all of the battle results had
not yet reached the king. We can almost sense his anxiety at receiving the
rest of the news. It is one thing for a united empire to attack another, but an
entirely different ball game when factions within an empire battle.

**Then the king asks Esther what else she wishes him to do. How does she
respond in Esther 9:13?**

Scripture does not celebrate or condemn Esther's choice to add another day to the Jewish massacre of their enemies. It is simply stated as fact. Perhaps we even question Esther's motives when she requests the king to order such willful carnage. Dare we label her actions as revenge-motivated?

We have seen through Haman's actions that hateful pride is taught. He held on to a generations-old grudge between the Benjaminites and Amalekites to justify his attack on Mordecai and the Jews. Perhaps the ten sons of Haman were killed so that there was no one left to carry on their father's legacy of hateful pride. We can only speculate.

Scholars almost unanimously condemn Esther for requesting another day of carnage, assuming that her newfound power had gone to her head. Her actions sound barbaric, especially by today's standards. However, such warfare tactics are seen in other places in the Old Testament.

Esther's actions demonstrate just how numerous and serious the enemies of the Jews were. It took drastic steps to save the Jewish people from Satan's desire to annihilate them. It took two days in Susa because the enemies were so numerous. Similarly, in Joshua 10, God made the sun stand still for twenty-four hours so that none of Israel's enemies could escape the battle.

Leaders would prolong a battle to ensure they had uncovered all of their enemies from hiding so the enemies could not cause future problems.

Read 1 Samuel 31:1–3.

Even though the tables are turned in those 1 Samuel verses and the enemies are victorious, the Philistines chased down the Israelites so that they could root out Saul. They wanted to ensure that he could never again wage battle.

Whether or not Esther was justified in her quest, one startling fact is clear: *Not one Jew is listed among the casualties.* God's invisible hand of providence is beautifully displayed as He completely protects His chosen people so that *not one life was lost.*

Despite the violence described in Esther 9, the author specifically mentions three separate occasions when the Jews left their enemy's plunder untouched. Regarding plunder, write out the phrase that is repeated at the end of Esther 9:10, 15, and 16:

The author believed it was important to stress three times that God's people were not fighting over plunder, money, or other tangible benefit. They knew fighting solely for material gain was a hollow prize. God's people were fighting to defend their right to live and their very way of life. The Jews did not take plunder that God did not authorize, because they had experienced in the past what happened when they plundered on their own accord.

Read 1 Samuel 15:17–23.

When Saul disobeyed the Lord and kept the spoils of war, what happened?

In this instance, God did not give permission for His people to plunder their enemies, only to destroy them. Yet Saul thought that he knew better than God. This story is where some of the Amalekites escaped destruction and continued to exist. Haman was an Amalekite (Agagite, after King Agag). Perhaps if Saul had obeyed God's command, Haman would never have existed to wreak havoc in the Book of Esther.

There were many occasions where God commanded His people to take plunder, including Ai, the town they captured after Jericho (Joshua 8:2). Further, Exodus 12:36 states that the Israelites plundered the Egyptians at God's command (first commanded by God in Exodus 11:2–3).

In Esther's situation, the Persian Jews did not plunder the Persians in order to demonstrate that their sole motive in the killings was self-defense—not greed. In that day, it was unusual for a victor not to take the spoils—so it would stand out and be remembered.

Also, the sheer number of enemies killed indicates precisely how many enemies there were, enemies who undoubtedly would have killed and plundered the Israelites if given the chance.

The Persian Jews made sure that they did not commit the same mistake as Saul. They left the plunder where it was and simply rejoiced that God had spared their lives.

Have you ever caused difficulty in someone's life to gain some kind of plunder, such as a promotion, wealth, or other benefit? If so, what was it, and what happened?

Plunder is not promised to us in this life. Yes, God provides many blessings to us, but we are not entitled to them by default. Jesus promised us that in this world we *will* have trouble; however, He came to overcome it (John 16:33).

We close this lesson with the climactic battle finally over. God's people have emerged victorious. Now, it's time to celebrate! I hope you stay tuned for the party, sister!

DAY 4
The Feast of Purim

> And Mordecai recorded these things and sent letters to all
> the Jews who were in all the provinces of King Ahasuerus,
> both near and far, obliging them to keep the fourteenth
> day of the month Adar and also the fifteenth day of the
> same, year by year, as the days on which the Jews got
> relief from their enemies, and as the month that had been
> turned for them from sorrow into gladness and from
> mourning into a holiday.
>
> (Esther 9:20–22a)

Today the curtain lifts to reveal a colorful, jubilant celebration complete with balloons, streamers, and mile-high cake! God divinely orchestrated and brought His people victory; now it is time to celebrate His goodness and gift of life.

Read Esther 9:17–32.
What stands out to you in those passages?

The overarching theme of the Book of Esther is God's deliverance of His people from destruction, and the result is a wonderful celebration known as the Feast of Purim. This feast is not mentioned in Leviticus 23 or anywhere else in Mosaic Law. However, were it not for the Book of Esther, we would not know how today's Purim celebrations came about.

The Feast of Purim was established to commemorate God's deliverance of His chosen people through the courageous bravery of Esther and her cousin Mordecai. According to Esther 9:20–21, on what days and for how long was the celebration to occur?

They were to celebrate on those specific days year after year. Those celebrations still happen today in Jewish communities all around the world. In Esther 9:22, what was the reason for this celebration?

God had turned their sorrow into gladness! That begs the question: Do you take time to celebrate what God has accomplished on your behalf?

When is the last time you celebrated?

How did you celebrate?

After I wrap up filming a Bible study series as it heads into post-production, the one thing that I look forward to is celebrating with those who made it happen. I book a table at a local restaurant that's big enough to invite the camera crew, pastoral reviewers, host location leaders, and dear friends to celebrate what God allowed us to accomplish together. We cannot get too busy with life that we forget to celebrate what God is doing among us!

Esther 9:22 is a beautiful picture of community. What did festival-goers usually do?

Although not mentioned in Scripture outside of the Book of Esther, Purim has been faithfully celebrated by the Jewish people from the time of Esther until today. Today, Purim is a carnival-type atmosphere where festival-goers dress up as characters from the book. An important part of Purim is the tradition of charitable giving of food and drink to the poor. Isn't that just like God not to forget those in need when we enjoy plenty?

How do you see similar generosity and fellowship in Acts 2:42–47?

God is full of grace and generosity and commands us to be likewise. As we see Jesus do time and again in the New Testament, we are to help those in need and generously share the blessings God has given us.

In Esther 9:27–28, how were the Jews to remember Purim?

Purim is one of only two festivals designated apart from Mosaic Law that is still celebrated by Jewish people today. The Festival of Lights (Hanukkah) is the other (John 10:22).

The Book of Esther is contained in the Megilloth, or "five scrolls," appearing in the third part of the Jewish canon. During five special occasions in the Jewish year, rabbis read aloud five particular Old Testament books in the synagogue: Lamentations, Ruth, Song of Solomon, Esther, and Ecclesiastes. Esther is read during Purim, Song of Songs is read during Passover, Ruth is read at Pentecost, Lamentations is read at the Ninth of Av, and Ecclesiastes is read at the Feast of Tabernacles.

Christ followers may be familiar with all of those Jewish festivals except perhaps the Ninth of Av. It is the Jewish day of mourning that commemorates the nation's historic catastrophes that happened on that day, such as when both temples were destroyed and when both world wars began.

In Esther 9:29–32, Esther leveraged her authority to institute an ongoing celebration of God's deliverance of His people. Is it any wonder that she is still celebrated as a heroine? What ongoing occasions do Christians celebrate each year?

Christ's birth at Christmas, His death on Good Friday, and His glorious resurrection on Easter Sunday are a few of the most well-known and beloved.

Starting all the way back in the ninth century AD, the thirteenth day of Adar (the day before the Feast of Purim begins) is set aside as a time of fasting (rather than the full three-day fast that Esther endured), usually beginning an hour before sunrise until an hour after sunset the next day.

The Feast of Purim was likely the impetus for including the Book of Esther in the *Tanakh* (or Jewish canon). Scholars generally agree that one of the main purposes, if not *the* main purpose, of the Book of Esther is to explain the origin of the Feast of Purim. Outside of Scripture, the earliest reference to the Feast of Purim is found in 2 Maccabees 15:36.

One of the foods that Purim celebrants enjoy today is called a "Haman pocket." Called *hamantashen* (or *oznei Haman* in Hebrew), these three-cornered pastry treats filled with poppy seeds (or other fillings) seem to have originated from a myth that the pastries celebrate the cutting off of the wicked man's ears before he was hanged. No historical credit is given to such an occurrence; however, Jewish people enjoy *hamantashen* each year during Purim.

Even today, Haman's name holds notoriety. At modern Purim festivals, each time Haman's name is read from the scroll of the Book of Esther, celebrants boo or use noisemakers to drown out Haman's name. Perhaps Christians should start booing and using noisemakers any time Satan's name is mentioned when Scripture is read!

When God faithfully brings you through a hard situation, do you take

time to remember and celebrate how He guided you through? How?

Do you have any tangible item that represents how you commemorate God's faithfulness in that situation? If so, what is it, and why did you choose that particular item?

Today, Esther is a popular name for Jewish girls. In fact, the largest international Jewish women's organization (founded by Henrietta Szold in 1912) was named Hadassah in honor of the biblical Esther.

As the party comes to a close as we end this lesson, we marvel at what God can accomplish through the faithfulness of His people. No other woman besides Esther in all of God's Word wrote with such authority to sanction and inaugurate a Jewish religious practice that still exists today.

We thank God and celebrate the importance of godly women such as Sarah and Hannah as models for motherhood. Esther's significance to the Jewish people, however, did not come as a mother, but as a queen.

DAY 5
The Wisdom of Mordecai

> For Mordecai the Jew was second in rank to King Aha-
> suerus, and he was great among the Jews and popular with
> the multitude of his brothers, for he sought the welfare of
> his people and spoke peace to all his people.
>
> (Esther 10:3)

Chapter 10 ends much as Chapter 1 began—pointing to the greatness, wealth, and splendor of King Ahasuerus. He begins by adding to his treasure chest by an "imposed tax," which means the king taxed the people.

Read Esther 10:1–3.

Esther 10:2 mentions the "Book of the Chronicles of the kings of Media and Persia." As we learned at the beginning of our study, archaeologists have yet to discover such a book.

Do you believe this casts doubt on the events of the Book of Esther? Why or why not?

According to Esther 10:3, why was Mordecai considered great among the Jews?

Mordecai was not only spared but was finally elevated as a respected leader. Thinking back over our study, what character traits did he possess that would have made Mordecai successful in that position?

When you decide to follow a leader, what character traits are important to you?

Mordecai possessed character traits that serve any leader well: honesty, trustworthiness, strength, tenacity, and most important, unwavering faith in God.

What position or ranking does Mordecai hold in the empire according to Esther 10:3?

Ahasuerus placed Mordecai in Haman's spot of second-in-command, or prime minister, over the entire Persian Empire. Another of God's faithful servants rose to a similar prominent position in a different land long before Mordecai: Joseph.

Born to Jacob and Rachael out of their great love, Joseph was Jacob's favorite child who was sold into slavery by his jealous brothers. He spent years in slavery and imprisonment until, in God's perfect timing, Joseph was called from his prison cell to come before Pharaoh and interpret the monarch's dream.

To which position did Pharaoh elevate Joseph in Genesis 41:39–40?

Even though Esther is not mentioned in this story's epilogue, she is the celebrated heroine of this Persian drama. There are no miracles in the Book of Esther, yet our Mighty Designer and Coordinator orchestrated the miraculous rescue of His people. The faithfulness of one woman and one man made all the difference.

No matter what you are facing, God still sits on His throne. The divine Architect of our lives guides us by His perfect love to accomplish His perfect purposes in His perfect timing.

Esther's crowning achievement was not wearing a crown, but in bowing low to save a people brought low in the world. She began this drama as a worldly trophy wife, but she ended it as a courageous, godly heroine. Esther started this story as an orphan with limited opportunities. You may believe that your opportunities are insignificant and your circle of influence is small, but with God as King over your life, nothing is impossible.

God's chosen people comprise a significant character in this drama, yet they are not given a speaking part. They hover ever present in the shadows onstage so that the beneficiaries of Esther's courage and bravery are never forgotten.

As we wrap up our journey through the Book of Esther, how shall we view it? Is it merely a moral tale about standing up against adversity in this life? Or rather, is it a Gospel-centered missive pointing to our reliance on Christ, our Redeemer, who secured our deliverance on a wooden cross?

Write your thoughts here.

As God promised Abraham way back in Genesis 12:3, "I will bless those who bless you, and him who dishonors you I will curse, and in you all the families of the earth shall be blessed." In every generation, in every century, God is faithful.

The Book of Esther challenges us to listen to God carefully to discern when He has brought us to a specific place and specific point in life "for such a time as this" (Esther 4:14).

As we reach the end of our study on the Book of Esther, list three things God has taught you or ways He has inspired you through her story.

1.

2.

3.

The Book of Esther touches us to the core because it teaches us how to navigate a society hostile to God and His Gospel. There are millions of Christians scattered across the globe awaiting the Lord's return. Even though He is with us every moment of every day, He is usually hidden by the ordinary, the best place where extraordinary can hide.

In a world hostile to the Gospel, I pray that God provides us with "eyes to see" His hand and masterful providence in our everyday circumstances. Though Esther hid her Jewishness and faith, the triumph of God's kingdom does not depend on our faulty faithfulness. Yet God draws us close to teach us, guide us, and humble us for the journey ahead.

You may feel like a nameless face in a blur of women, but God knows you by name. He knows every hair on your head. He wipes every tear from your eyes. He knows every longing of your mind and every desire of your heart.

And like Esther, He will mold and shape you into the woman of courage that He needs you to be. After all, dear friend, you are a daughter of the King!

God's blessings, dear sister, as you have stuck with this entire study! I pray that God continues to draw you into His Word to enrich your life and strengthen you to live a life of courage for the sake of Christ *for such a time as this.*

ACKNOWLEDGMENTS

It takes a village to produce a book, and this one was no different. In particular, I would like to acknowledge:

- My Family: Thank you for your unwavering love and support, even when I missed time with you to research and write. Cheers to the Quad Squad! I love you so much.

- Rev. Doug Dommer: Thank you for generously sharing the brilliant mind and spiritual wisdom that God has given you. Even when this study felt daunting, your encouragement made a huge difference. I love you like a brother.

- Belinda Burmeister: Thank you for offering beautiful insights and editorial suggestions as you deciphered each raw chapter. Your godly friendship and love for Jesus is a precious blessing in my life. I love you, dear sister in Christ.

- Rev. Tim Carter: Each time I typed the word *humility* in these pages, God brought you to mind. Thank you for being a living example of godly humility and a dear brother in Christ.

- Ori Katzir: Thank you for being the best tour guide in Israel and answering my never-ending questions about Jewish culture, Hebrew language, and the Book of Esther. Your personal and scholarly insights made this a culturally rich study. I thank God for you and treasure our friendship.

- Peggy Kuethe: Your incredible editing skills and spiritual insights truly took this study to a whole 'notha level. I hold our friendship closely. I thank God for the special bond He has forged between us, dear friend.

- Janetta Messmer: Even in the wee hours of the morning, your mad editing skills never failed. Thank you for late nights and commitment beyond comparison as the deadline loomed. I love you, Hoot!

- Rachelle Gardner: The best agent any author could ask for! You are a huge blessing in my life.

- The CPH Dream Team: Your creativity and innovative ideas inspire me. Thank you for dreaming big and letting me hitch a ride. Working with you is truly a joyful blessing!

- And to each of you who offered encouragement, wisdom and prayers along this study's journey, you made all the difference. Thank you!

ENDNOTES

1. Sayce, *An Introduction to the Books of Ezra, Nehemiah, and Esther,* 120.

2. *Lutheran Bible Companion, Volume 1: Introduction and Old Testament,* 475.

3. TheTorah.com, "Newly Deciphered Qumran Scroll Revealed to Be Megillat Esther," Dr. Rabbi Asher Tov-Lev, thetorah.com/article/newly-deciphered-qumran-scroll-revealed-to-be-megillat-esther. Accessed September 28, 2020.

4. *Lutheran Bible Companion, Volume 1: Introduction and Old Testament,* 460.

5. James Russell Lowell, "*The Present Crisis.*" poets.org/poem/present-crisis. In the public domain. Accessed March 20, 2020.

6. *Esther, For Such a Time as This,* 9.

7. Katzir, *Book of Esther, n.p.*

8. Pyle, *Forgiveness: Received from God, Extended to Others,* 97.

9. Lifelight, *Ruth/Esther, Leaders Guide,* 31.

10. Katzir, *Book of Esther,* n.p.

11. *The Apocrypha: The Lutheran Edition with Notes,* 235.

12. W. W. Wiersbe, *Be Committed,* 110.

13. Sayce, *An Introduction to the Books of Ezra, Nehemiah, and Esther,* 114.

14. Katzir, *Book of Esther,* n.p.

15. *The Lutheran Study Bible,* 792.

16. *The Apocrypha: The Lutheran Edition with Notes,* 233.

17. *The Apocrypha: The Lutheran Edition with Notes,* 234.

18. *The Apocrypha: The Lutheran Edition with Notes,* 228.

19. *The Apocrypha: The Lutheran Edition with Notes,* 234.

20. EchosandReflections.org, "*Those Who Dared to Rescue.*" Lesson 7, Rescuers and Non-Jewish Resistance, quoting Elie Wiesel, in Carol Rittner and Sandra Meyers, *Courage to Care—Rescuers of Jews during the Holocaust* (New York University Press, 1986), 2. echoesandreflections.org/wp-content/uploads/2014/04/EchoesAndReflections_Lesson_Seven_InformationalText-ThoseWhoDaredToRescue.pdf. Accessed April 2, 2020.

21. Elie Wiesel, Acceptance Speech. NobelPrize.org. Nobel Media AB 2020. Thu. 2 Apr 2020. nobelprize.org/prizes/peace/1986/wiesel/26054-elie-wiesel-acceptance-speech-1986/

22. *The Apocrypha: The Lutheran Edition with Notes,* 235.

23. Torrey, *How to Obtain Fullness of Power in Christian Life and Service,* 59.

24. *The Apocrypha: The Lutheran Edition with Notes,* 238.

25. Spurgeon, *Providence—As Seen in the Book of Esther,* Sermon No. 1201.

REFERENCES

Academy of Achievement. "*Elie Wiesel.*" *achievement.org/achiever/elie-wiesel/* (accessed April 2, 2020).

The Apocrypha: The Lutheran Edition with Notes. St. Louis: Concordia Publishing House, 2012.

Companion Bible: The Authorized Version of 1611, Being the Authorized Version of 1611 with Structures and Critical and Explanatory Notes with 198 Appendixes. Grand Rapids: Kregel Publications, 1999.

Esther: For Such a Time as This. St. Louis: Concordia Publishing House, 2008.

George, Elizabeth. *Becoming a Woman of Integrity: Esther.* Eugene, Oreg.: Harvest House Publishers, 2011.

Greidanus, Sidney. *Preaching Christ from the Old Testament. Grand Rapids:* Wm. B. Eerdmans, 1999, 120, footnote 34.

Gordis, Robert. *Megillat Esthe.* New York: Ktav, 1974, 13–14.

"*Hammurabi Biography.*" *Biography.com.* A&E Television Networks, last modified August 21, 2019. biography.com/political-figure/Hammurabi (accessed January 30, 2020).

Holocaust Encyclopedia. "*First They Came for the Socialists.*" United States Holocaust Memorial Museum, Washington DC. encyclopedia.ushmm.org/content/en/article/martin-niemoeller-first-they-came-for-the-socialists (accessed March 20, 2020).

Hirst, K. Kris. "*The Royal Road of the Achaemenids: International Highway of Darius the Great.*" *ThoughtCo.* thoughtco.com/royal-road-of-the-achaemenids-172590 (accessed February 26, 2020).

Jobes, Karen H. *The NIV Application Commentary: Esther.* Grand Rapids:

Zondervan Publishing House, 1999.

Katzir, Ori. *Book of Esther.* Scholarly white paper on the Book of Esther from a native Israeli Jewish, political perspective. Referenced and used by permission.

King, L. W. "*The Code of Hammurabi.*" Yale University, Lillian Goodman Law Library, 2008. avalon.law.yale.edu/ancient/hamframe.asp (accessed January 30, 2020).

LCMS Commission on Theology and Church Relations (CTCR). *The Royal Priesthood.* 2018files.lcms.org/wl/?id=sKchZQlIvrVVAJ6JqTkyqmW2FUx9NQZo (accessed March 26, 2020).

Lendering, Jona. "*Herodotus' Histories.*" *Livius.org.* www.livius.org/articles/person/herodotus/herodotus-histories/ (accessed February 28, 2020).

Life Application Study Bible. Carol Stream, Ill.: Tyndale House, 2005.

Life Application Bible Commentary, 1–2 Timothy and Titus. Carol Stream: Tyndale House 1993.

LifeLight: *Ruth/Esther, Leaders Guide.* St. Louis: Concordia Publishing House, 2008.

LifeLight: *Ruth/Esther, Study Guide.* St. Louis: Concordia Publishing House, 2008.

Livingstone, E. A., and F. L. Cross. *The Oxford Dictionary of the Christian Church. Logos.com.* app.logos.com/books/holocaust (accessed March 30, 2020).

Lutheran Bible Companion. Volume 1: Introduction and Old Testament. St. Louis: Concordia Publishing House, 2009.

The Lutheran Study Bible. St. Louis: Concordia Publishing House, 2009.

MacArthur, John. *Ruth & Esther: Women of Faith, Bravery and Hope.* Nashville: W

Publishing Group, 2000.

Moore, Beth. *Esther: It's Tough Being a Woman.* Wheaton, Ill.: Lifeway Press, 2008.

NIV Cultural Backgrounds Study Bible. Grand Rapids: Zondervan, 2016, 799–813.

NLT Study Bible. Carol Stream, Ill.: Tyndale House Publishers, 2008, 834–47.

NRSV Journal. The Word Bible with Apocrypha/Deuterocanonical Books. Grand Rapids: Zondervan, 1989, pp. 1221–33.

Pell, Patty. *Esther: Character under Pressure.* Downers Grove, Ill.: InterVarsity Press, 2002.

Peterson, Eugene H. *Esther: Finding Yourself in Times of Trouble.* Carol Stream, Ill.: Tyndale House Publishers, 2017.

Pyle, Donna. *Forgiveness: Received from God, Extended to Others.* St. Louis: Concordia Publishing House, 2016.

Pyle, Donna. *Perseverance.* St. Louis: Concordia Publishing House, 2019.

Sayce, A. H. *An Introduction to the Books of Ezra, Nehemiah, and Esther.* London: The Religious Trust Society, 1893.

Spurgeon, C. H. *Providence—As Seen in the Book of Esther.* Sermon No. 1201, November 1, 1874. *SpurgeonGems.org.* Spurgeongems.org/sermon/chs1201.pdf (accessed March 18, 2020).

Torrey, R. A. *How to Obtain Fullness of Power in Christian Life and Service.* New York: Fleming H. Revell, 1897.

Walton, John H. *Cultural Background Study Bible (NKJV).* New York: HarperCollins Publishers, 2019.

Walton, John H. *The IVP Bible Background Commentary: Old Testament.*

Downers Grove, Ill.: InterVarsity Press, 2001, 483–90.

"What Happened on the Ninth of Av?" chabad.org. chabad.org/library/article_cdo/aid/946703/jewish/What-Happened-on-the-Ninth-of-Av.htm (accessed March 3, 2020).

"Who Was Henrietta Szold?" MyJewishLearning.org. www.myjewishlearning.com/article/henrietta-szold-1860-1945/ (accessed March 3, 2020).

Wiersbe, W. W. *Be Committed.* Wheaton, Ill.: Victor Books, 1993.

Zuck, Roy B. *The Speaker's Quote Book.* Grand Rapids: Kregel Publications, 1997.